THE ULTIMATE FOOTBALL TRIVIA CHALLENGE

OVER 600 QUIZ QUESTIONS FOR
DIE-HARD FOOTBALL FANS

HANK PATTON

ISBN: 979-8-89095-057-4

Copyright © 2025 by Curious Press

ALL RIGHTS RESERVED

No part of this book may be reproduced, stored in a retrieval system, or transmitted in any form or by any means, electronic, mechanical, photocopying, recording, scanning, or otherwise, without the prior written permission of the publisher.

CONTENTS

CHAPTER 1: 4
    Chapter 1 Answers: 7
CHAPTER 2: 9
    Chapter 2 Answers: 12
CHAPTER 3: 14
    Chapter 3 Answers: 17
CHAPTER 4: 19
    Chapter 4 Answers: 22
CHAPTER 5: 24
    Chapter 5 Answers: 27
CHAPTER 6: 29
    Chapter 6 Answers: 32
CHAPTER 7: 34
    Chapter 7 Answers: 37
CHAPTER 8: 39
    Chapter 8 Answers: 42
CHAPTER 9: 44
    Chapter 9 Answers: 47
CHAPTER 10: 49
    Chapter 10 Answers: 52
CHAPTER 11: 54
    Chapter 11 Answers: 57
CHAPTER 12: 59
    Chapter 12 Answers: 62

CHAPTER 13:	64
Chapter 13 Answers:	67
CHAPTER 14:	69
Chapter 14 Answers:	72
CHAPTER 15:	74
Chapter 15 Answers:	77
CHAPTER 16:	79
Chapter 16 Answers:	82
CHAPTER 17:	84
Chapter 17 Answers:	87
CHAPTER 18:	89
Chapter 18 Answers:	92
CHAPTER 19:	94
Chapter 19 Answers:	97
CHAPTER 20:	101
Chapter 20 Answers:	104
CHAPTER 21:	108
Chapter 21 Answers:	111
CHAPTER 22:	114
Chapter 22 Answers:	117
CHAPTER 23:	120
Chapter 23 Answers:	123
CHAPTER 24:	126
Chapter 24 Answers:	129
CHAPTER 25:	132
Chapter 25 Answers:	135
CHAPTER 26:	138

Chapter 26 Answers: 141
CHAPTER 27: 144
    Chapter 27 Answers: 147
CHAPTER 28: 149
    Chapter 28 Answers: 152
CHAPTER 29: 154
    Chapter 29 Answers: 157
CHAPTER 30: 159
    Chapter 30 Answers: 162
CHAPTER 31: 164
    Chapter 31 Answers: 167
CHAPTER 32: 169
    Chapter 32 Answers: 172
CHAPTER 33: 174
    Chapter 33 Answers: 177
CHAPTER 34: 180
    Chapter 34 Answers: 181

ATTENTION:

DO YOU WANT MY FUTURE BOOKS AT HEAVY DISCOUNTS AND EVEN FOR FREE?

HEAD OVER TO WWW.SECRETREADS.COM AND JOIN MY SECRET BOOK CLUB!

INTRODUCTION

Football is a sport with a substantial history in the United States. With over 160 years of battles taking place on the gridiron, it has arguably become one of the most entertaining and captivating sport in the country.

Football is a game that grew quickly, and as the game grew, the rules changed to meet the challenges of new and exciting players coming to play. While colleges were the first to adopt the game, the professional scene quickly followed, and people all across the country were more than happy to watch.

Modern football is fast and sophisticated, and it features competitors that are not only the most athletic the game has ever seen, but they are often the smartest as well. Professional football has never been more competitive or popular as it is today.

With football's popularity, it can be difficult to explain where the game came from and who created the cornerstones that support today's teams and players. Do you know who set the early records and helped teams win championships before the Super Bowl even came into existence?

The first few chapters of this trivia book will be the most challenging, as they cover the earliest days of the game. Players, teams, and leagues unknown to today's fans will be the topic, testing even the best football historians.

Each team's best players will also be featured in the book, ensuring that any football fan will see the biggest names in their favorite team's history.

The first questions you need to consider are: Do you have the football knowledge to pass each of the challenging chapters in this book? Can you conquer every category and prove your football supremacy?

Get your football friends or family together, or give this book a shot on your own, and prepare for a great football trivia challenge! Will you hit the open receiver down field, check down to the safe play, or get sacked by these difficult questions?

Give it your best and be ready for the blitz!

CHAPTER 1:

FOOTBALL'S INVENTION AND EARLY DAYS

1. Which athlete from Yale is credited with helping football diverge from soccer and rugby?
   A. Walter Camp
   B. Glenn "Pop" Warner
   C. Eddie Cochems
   D. Knute Rockne

2. In which year was the rule establishing the line of scrimmage, and the snap from center to quarterback, instituted?
   A. 1878
   B. 1880
   C. 1882
   D. 1884

3. True or False: Teams initially abused the new line of scrimmage rules to slow down the game.

4. True or False: Referees with whistles were mandated beginning in 1887.

5. When one feature of the modern game was finally legalized, it marked the biggest shift away from rugby and soccer, making the game unique. Which was it?
   A. Interceptions
   B. Blocking
   C. Screen passes
   D. Tackling below the waist

6. In 1883, a touchdown was worth how many points?
   A. One
   B. Two
   C. Three

D. Four

7. True or False: A field goal was worth more than any other score until 1898.

8. True or False: The original conversion after a touchdown was worth double the number of points of the touchdown itself.

9. A point-after try was reduced from four points to two in which year?

    A. 1883
    B. 1898
    C. 1904
    D. 1912

10. Walter Camp selected which of these from 1889 to 1924?

    A. College Football MVP
    B. National Champions
    C. Game of the Year
    D. All-American team

11. True or False: Walter Camp played quarterback during his time at Yale.

12. True or False: Walter Camp also invented scoring by way of a safety.

13. Which college team was the first to use the "Flying Wedge" technique, where blocking players locked arms to form a running barricade?

    A. Yale
    B. Harvard
    C. Princeton
    D. Rutgers

14. Princeton played against which team on November 6, 1869, considered the first American football game ever?

    A. Harvard
    B. Yale
    C. Rutgers
    D. McGill

15. True or False: President Theodore Roosevelt demanded changes to football's rules after 19 players died in 1905.

16. True or False: The Oneida Football Club is considered the oldest known football club in the country.

17. Which of these universities was the first school west of Pennsylvania to create a college football team?

    A. University of Illinois
    B. University of Chicago
    C. University of Michigan
    D. Ohio State University

18. October 26, 1895 is allegedly the date of the first ever _____?

    A. Fake punt
    B. Forward pass
    C. Option pitch
    D. Fumble touchdown

CHAPTER 1 ANSWERS:

1. A. Walter Camp. He is considered the "Father of American Football."
2. B. 1880. The center used to snap the ball with his foot, not his hand.
3. True. Princeton University simply made slow progress as there were no rules establishing downs.
4. False. Referees were mandated in 1887, but whistles were not added until 1889.
5. B. Blocking. Teams were trying while it was illegal, but it eventually became part of the game.
6. B. Two. Besides a safety, it was worth the fewest points of any score.
7. True. It was originally worth five points.
8. True. It was worth four points.
9. A. 1883. The first set of rules did not even last a year.
10. D. All-American team. A foundation in Camp's name continues this tradition.
11. False. He played halfback.
12. True. It was a significant departure from rugby rules.
13. B. Harvard. It only lasted a few years before being outlawed due to safety concerns.
14. C. Rutgers. Princeton would lose that game, 6-4.
15. True. It led to the formation of the NCAA.
16. True. It was established in 1862 for Boston's prep school students.
17. C. University of Michigan. They defeated Racine College 1-0 in May 1879.
18. B. Forward pass. It happened on accident in a game between Georgia and North Carolina.

Did You Know?

Professional football in the United States began in 1892, a couple of decades after the game emerged from the college level.

CHAPTER 2:
THE EARLY COLLEGE SCENE

1. In the first game ever played in the state of Kansas, which college team beat the University of Kansas 22-9?

   A. Baker University
   B. Vanderbilt University
   C. Washington and Lee College
   D. University of Virginia

2. When Auburn University created their first football program in 1892, they played which team in their first game?

   A. University of Florida
   B. University of Pennsylvania
   C. Vanderbilt University
   D. University of Georgia

3. True or False: The 1900 Stanford University team outscored their opponents 154-20.

4. True or False: Michigan won 56 straight games from 1901 to 1905.

5. Many teams on the west coast moved away from football to which sport?

   A. Soccer
   B. Rugby union
   C. Baseball
   D. Field hockey

6. In a game known as the "Hampden Park Blood Bath," how many players ended up crippled?

   A. Three
   B. Four
   C. Five
   D. Six

7. True or False: Georgia fullback Richard Von Albade Gammon died from a concussion while on the field in 1897.

8. True or False: In 1906, the forward pass became a legal play, changing the game forever.

9. After the forward pass was made legal, which team's quarterback was credited with completing the first one?

    A. Carroll College
    B. University of Syracuse
    C. Saint Louis University
    D. McGill University

10. The "South's Oldest Rivalry" is a matchup between which two teams?

    A. Georgia and Auburn
    B. North Carolina and Virginia
    C. Texas and California
    D. Alabama and Auburn

11. True or False: Alex Moffat was considered early football's greatest kicker, back in the 1880s.

12. True or False: Harvard player Arthur Cumnock invented the first chin guard, helping make the sport safer.

13. Rutgers played which team in November of 1872, marking the first time in history a game ended in a scoreless draw?

    A. New York University
    B. Columbia
    C. Princeton
    D. Yale

14. Which team was the first to score 100 points in a game?

    A. Harvard
    B. Princeton
    C. Yale
    D. Rutgers

15. True or False: The first time a player used a helmet was in 1902, in a game between Army and Navy.

16. True or False: The first Black player selected as an All-American was William H. Lewis, in 1892.

17. Which school broke Michigan's 56-game winning streak in a game dubbed "The First Greatest Game of the Century" in 1905?

    A. Michigan State
    B. Penn State
    C. Ohio State
    D. Chicago

18. North Carolina had their only undefeated season in which year?

    A. 1898
    B. 1899
    C. 1900
    D. 1901

CHAPTER 2 ANSWERS:

1. A. Baker University. The game was played on November 22, 1890.
2. D. University of Georgia. Auburn won that game, 10-0.
3. True. They had a 7-2-1 record that year.
4. True. They outscored opponents 2,831-40 during that streak.
5. B. Rugby union. The east coast teams considered the west coast teams to be inferior, so they did not follow the trend away from football.
6. B. Four. Harvard and Yale would not play each other again for three years.
7. False. He died later in hospital but the event caused many teams to temporarily suspend their football programs.
8. True. It was an effort to make the game safer.
9. C. Saint Louis University. Bradbury Robinson completed two passes, one for a touchdown.
10. B. North Carolina and Virginia. It's not to be confused with the "Deep South's Oldest Rivalry."
11. True. He developed the spiral kick and invented the drop kick.
12. False. He invented the first nose guard. He also began the tradition of spring practice.
13. B. Columbia. Scoring was rare before the forward pass.
14. C. Yale. They defeated Dartmouth 113-0 in October of 1884.
15. False. It took place in 1893.
16. True. He played for Harvard.
17. D. Chicago. They won 2-0.
18. A. 1898. They were 9-0 on the season.

DID YOU KNOW?

The 1899 Sewanee Tigers were 12-0 and outscored their opponents in total by 322-10.

CHAPTER 3:

COLLEGE FOOTBALL AFTER 1910

1. True or False: The requirement for seven offensive players on the line of scrimmage came around in 1910.

2. True or False: Amos Alonzo Stagg is credited with inventing the huddle and the pre-snap formation shift.

3. The first roughing-the-passer or kicker penalty was implemented in which year, reacting to the increase in forward passes?

    A. 1914
    B. 1916
    C. 1918
    D. 1920

4. Field goals went down to three points in 1909, but how many years later did touchdowns increase to six points?

    A. Three
    B. Four
    C. Five
    D. Six

5. True or False: Sportswriter Grantland Rice is credited with helping popularize college football by giving unique nicknames to the best players.

6. True or False: Grantland Rice famously named Notre Dame's linemen the "Seven Blocks of Granite."

7. Jim Thorpe won the 1912 intercollegiate championship in which sport?

    A. Track and field
    B. Ballroom dancing
    C. Lacrosse
    D. Baseball

8. In the 1916 Rose Bowl Game, which team defeated Brown?

A. Oregon
   B. Gonzaga
   C. Washington State
   D. Whitman

9. True or False: The first radio broadcast of a college football game was in 1919.

10. True or False: The first game with a halftime show that featured a marching band was in 1907.

11. College football made a rule in 1927 that required shifting offensive players to be still for one second before the snap, all because of which coach's complex offensive schemes?

    A. Jesse Harper
    B. Gil Dobie
    C. Walter Camp
    D. Knute Rockne

12. Which of these players was not a member of the 1924 Fighting Irish's "Four Horsemen"?

    A. Don Miller
    B. Jim Crowley
    C. John Mohardt
    D. Elmer Layden

13. True or False: Red Grange scored six touchdowns for Michigan, defeating Illinois in 1924.

14. True or False: The most lopsided game in college football history was a 222-0 win for Georgia Tech.

15. Which year's Rose Bowl is known as the "Game that changed the south"?

    A. 1925
    B. 1926
    C. 1927
    D. 1928

16. John Heisman coached several teams, but which one did he lead to a National Championship in 1917?

    A. Clemson

B. Auburn
C. Georgia Tech
D. Akron

17. True or False: Glenn "Pop" Warner is credited with inventing the three-point stance.

18. True or False: The 1919 Texas A&M Aggies were 10-0, and they did not allow their opponents to score at all.

CHAPTER 3 ANSWERS:

1. True. Interlocking to block was also removed from the sport.
2. True. He was a coach at the University of Chicago for several years. But Paul D. Hubbard, quarterback of Gallaudet University is also credited in the introduction.
3. A. 1914 Hopefully not too many quarterbacks or kickers were hurt before then.
4. A. Three. That change was made in 1912, and it remains unchanged to today.
5. True. He helped fans around the country get to know the players better.
6. False. That nickname belonged to the linemen of Fordham University.
7. B. Ballroom dancing. He seemingly excelled in everything.
8. C. Washington State. They won 14-0 to complete their undefeated season.
9. False. The first radio broadcast was in 1921, when West Virginia faced Pittsburgh on October 8.
10. True. Chicago defeated Illinois 42-6 that day.
11. D. Knute Rockne. He was the longtime coach at Notre Dame.
12. C. John Mohardt. Mohardt was quarterback for the team years earlier.
13. False. Grange scored those touchdowns for Illinois, defeating Michigan 39-14.
14. True. They defeated Cumberland in October of 1916.
15. B. 1926. Alabama defeated Washington, helping bring legitimacy to the southern schools.
16. C. Georgia Tech. They did not play in the Rose Bowl, though.
17. True. He also innovated the game by introducing shoulder pads and writing *Football for Coaches and Players*.
18. True. They were named National Champions retroactively.

DID YOU KNOW?

Knute Rockne died in a plane crash in 1931. His record was 105-12-5.

CHAPTER 4:

FIRST PRO LEAGUES

1. Before paying players was acceptable, Pudge Heffelfinger was secretly paid how much to play one game in November 1892?

    A. $100
    B. $500
    C. $680
    D. $750

2. The first attempt at a nationwide professional league, in 1902, went by what name?

    A. National Football League
    B. American Football Association
    C. Professional Football League
    D. Professional Football Association

3. True or False: The first National Football League lasted for five years before folding.

4. True or False: Two of the three teams in the league tied for first place after the six-game campaign.

5. Which NFL organization was founded first, back in 1895?

    A. New York Jets
    B. New York Giants
    C. Philadelphia Eagles
    D. Arizona Cardinals

6. The Ohio League formed in 1902 and had how many teams?

    A. 12
    B. 17
    C. 23
    D. 28

7. True or False: None of the Ohio League teams would survive more than ten years in the NFL.

8. True or False: A betting scandal ruined the reputation of the Canton Bulldogs of the Ohio League.

9. The World Series of Football lasted for how many seasons?

   A. One
   B. Two
   C. Three
   D. Four

10. Jim Thorpe was signed to which team in 1915?

    A. Akron East Ends
    B. Canton Bulldogs
    C. Dayton Triangles
    D. Elyria Athletics

11. True or False: The Massillon Tigers won five straight championships in the Ohio League.

12. True or False: Akron Parratt's Indians was the only team to win an Ohio League title with more than one loss.

13. The Ohio Valley League lasted for how many seasons, even after the NFL began to emerge?

    A. Three
    B. Four
    C. Five
    D. Six

14. Which Ohio Valley League team won three of the five league championships?

    A. Ashland Armco Yellowjackets
    B. Portsmouth Spartans
    C. Middletown Armco Blues
    D. Ironton Tanks

15. True or False: The Portsmouth Spartans won the final Ohio Valley League Championship and would later become the Chicago Bears.

16. True or False: In 1919, the New York Pro Football League became the first to use a playoff format instead of a one-game championship.

17. Which NYPFL team won the league's first two documented championships?
    A. Buffalo Cazenovias
    B. Lancaster
    C. Buffalo Oakdales
    D. Rochester Jeffersons
18. Which NYPFL team still exists today?
    A. Watertown Red & Black
    B. Syracuse Athletic Club
    C. Rochester Jeffersons
    D. Buffalo Niagaras

CHAPTER 4 ANSWERS:

1. B. $500. It was kept secret for several years as paying players was not allowed during this period of the sport.
2. A. National Football League. It has no connection to the modern NFL.
3. False. The league only lasted for one season.
4. True. The Pittsburgh Stars and Philadelphia Athletics both finished 3-2-1.
5. D. Arizona Cardinals. They began as the Morgan Athletic Club in Chicago.
6. C. 23. Most of them were in Ohio, but it helped form the NFL later.
7. True. The Dayton Triangles left after the 1926 season, the last remaining team.
8. True. It damaged professional football in the state for nearly a decade.
9. B. Two. It had five teams in the first season, six in the second.
10. B. Canton Bulldogs. He helped the team to two straight championships.
11. True. They won from 1903 to 1907.
12. True. Every other champion had either one or zero losses.
13. C. Five. It finally closed down when the Great Depression began.
14. D. Ironton Tanks. They won the first two, and the fourth championship.
15. False. They would become the Detroit Lions.
16. True. However, the league abandoned both playoffs and championships after that season.
17. C. Buffalo Oakdales. Records were spotty back then, but two other Buffalo teams also won titles.
18. A. Watertown Red & Blacks. They even won titles in 2021 and 2022, competing in the Empire Football League.

Did You Know?

Kanaweola Athletic Club hosted the first-ever night game in pro football, though there is little record of their existence after that game.

CHAPTER 5:
THE AMERICAN PROFESSIONAL FOOTBALL ASSOCIATION

1. True or False: Jim Thorpe was elected as the new league's first president in September 1920.

2. True or False: The APFA began with 14 teams and added four teams later that year.

3. Which of these teams was present at the beginning of the 1920 season?

    A. Detroit Heralds
    B. Decatur Staleys
    C. Buffalo All-Americans
    D. Chicago Tigers

4. The Akron Pros won how many games to claim the league's first championship?

    A. Six
    B. Seven
    C. Eight
    D. Nine

5. True or False: The league's first game was a 24-0 win for the Rock Island Independents.

6. True or False: Though the league had more than a dozen teams, only six finished the first season.

7. Which team joined in 1921 and holds the record for the longest use of a team name without changing it?

    A. Chicago Bears
    B. Green Bay Packers
    C. Detroit Lions
    D. Buffalo Bills

8. Which team won the 1921 Championship despite being sold and moved to a new city?

A. Buffalo All-Americans
   B. Chicago Staleys
   C. Canton Bulldogs
   D. Evansville Crimson Giants

9. True or False: The APFA changed their league name to the National Football League in June 24, 1922.

10. True or False: The Youngstown Patricians were supposed to be the 19th team during the 1922 season but folded before participating.

11. What was the salary cap for teams during the 1922 season (per game)?

    A. $900
    B. $1,100
    C. $1,200
    D. $1,400

12. Jim Thorpe coached which team himself, despite being the president of the league?

    A. Oorang Indians
    B. Racine Legion
    C. Milwaukee Badgers
    D. Toledo Maroons

13. True or False: Seven of the 20 teams participating in the 1923 season either folded or went on hiatus.

14. True or False: The Canton Bulldogs won the 1923 championship with an 11-0-1 record.

15. Though the Cleveland Bulldogs won the 1924 championship with an .875 winning percentage, which team had four more wins?

    A. Duluth Kelleys
    B. Frankford Yellow Jackets
    C. Racine Legion
    D. Buffalo Bisons

16. Which team was the 1925 league champions thanks to the Pottsville Maroons having their final win vacated?

    A. Detroit Panthers
    B. New York Giants
    C. Chicago Cardinals

D. Chicago Bears

17. True or False: The 1926 season was the first time the league attempted to travel south and west.

18. True or False: The American Football League challenged the NFL to a match between champions in 1926, but the NFL declined.

CHAPTER 5 ANSWERS:

1. True. He truly had a substantial impact on football in the United States.
2. True. The four extra teams included the Columbus Panhandles.
3. B. Decatur Staleys. They would eventually become today's Chicago Bears.
4. C. Eight. They tied three games, too.
5. False. They won 48-0 against a non-league team.
6. False. Only four teams finished the season.
7. B. Green Bay Packers. The Bears got their name one season later.
8. B. Chicago Staleys. They had nine wins along with Buffalo but won their second head-to-head matchup.
9. True. The league had 18 teams that season.
10. True. The same could also be said about the Philadelphia Union Quakers.
11. C. $1,200. New teams only had to pay an expansion fee of $500.
12. A. Oorang Indians. They finished the season with a 3-6 record.
13. True. This included the team coached by Jim Thorpe.
14. True. They only allowed 19 points in those games.
15. B. Frankford Yellow Jackets. They were 11-2-1, for an .846 winning percentage.
16. C. Chicago Cardinals. The controversy was revisited in 2003, but no change came from it.
17. True. They used traveling teams to reach other cities.
18. True. The NFL was unwilling to give any attention to the competing league.

Did You Know?

The league would shrink in 1927, from 22 teams down to 12.

CHAPTER 6:

FORMER NFL TEAMS

1. Out of the 49 defunct NFL teams throughout history, how many of them won championships before they folded?

   A. Three
   B. Four
   C. Five
   D. Six

2. The most recent team to fold was from which city?

   A. Dallas
   B. New York
   C. Baltimore
   D. Boston

3. True or False: Two teams folded in the league's first season, back in 1920.

4. True or False: More teams folded in 1926 than any other year.

5. Which of these teams that folded in 1921 was from the city of Tonawanda?

   A. Flyers
   B. Blues
   C. Maroons
   D. Kardex

6. Two teams folded in 1925: The Rochester Jeffersons and Rock Island Independents. In what year did these teams join the league?

   A. 1920
   B. 1922
   C. 1924
   D. 1925

7. True or False: The last founding teams to fold did so in 1929.

8. True or False: The Brooklyn Lions lasted longer than any other defunct team.

9. Of these teams that joined in 1921, which was the last to fold?

    A. Louisville Brecks/Colonels
    B. Evansville Crimson Giants
    C. Minneapolis Marines/Red Jackets
    D. Detroit Tigers

10. Which of these defunct teams did not win a championship?

    A. St. Louis All-Stars
    B. Frankford Yellow Jackets
    C. Cleveland Indians/Bulldogs
    D. Akron Pros/Indians

11. True or False: The Cincinnati Celts lasted four seasons before folding in 1924.

12. True or False: The city of Detroit has more defunct teams than any other.

13. Which city was briefly home to a team named the Eskimos?

    A. Vancouver
    B. Duluth
    C. Muncie
    D. Racine

14. Which of these cities did not have a team called the Tigers?

    A. Detroit
    B. Chicago
    C. Cleveland
    D. Toledo

15. True or False: The Staten Island Stapletons only lasted one season.

16. True or False: The Los Angeles Buccaneers lasted one season, in 1926.

17. Of the 12 founding teams, how many have made it to the present day?

    A. Zero
    B. One
    C. Two
    D. Three

18. A now-defunct team played one season in Orange, New Jersey, and one season in Newark, New Jersey. What was their team name?

   A. Yankees
   B. Giants
   C. Tornadoes
   D. Badgers

CHAPTER 6 ANSWERS:

1. C. Five. The last defunct team to accomplish the feat was the Providence Steam Roller, in 1925.
2. A. Dallas. The Dallas Texans folded in 1952.
3. True. The Chicago Tigers and Detroit Heralds both folded that year.
4. True. Twelve teams folded that season.
5. D. Kardex. It was named after a business that developed index cards.
6. A. 1920. They were the only two founding teams to fold that season.
7. True. The Dayton Triangles and Buffalo All-Americans both bowed out that year.
8. False. The Brooklyn Dodgers/Tigers lasted 14 seasons.
9. C. Minneapolis Marines/Red Jackets. They folded in 1930, though they did take a three-year hiatus in that time.
10. A. St. Louis All-Stars. They only played one season, in 1923.
11. False. The Celts played one season, in 1921.
12. True. They're the only city with four defunct teams.
13. B. Duluth. The team was also called the Kelleys, and they lasted five seasons.
14. D. Toledo. Their only team was named the Maroons.
15. False. The team lasted four seasons.
16. True. The travelling team experiment did not work as well as hoped.
17. C. Two. The Chicago Bears and Arizona Cardinals had their beginnings in 1920.
18. C. Tornadoes. They were 3-5-4 during the 1929 season, only scoring 35 points all year.

Did You Know?

An NFL expansion team needs 75% of the current teams' owners to approve their addition to the league.

CHAPTER 7:
THE 1930S

1. True or False: The Green Bay Packers won the 1930 championship, though the Bears had more wins.

2. True or False: The 1930 Packers clinched the championship thanks to a blocked PAT.

3. Which team canceled the last game of their season, allowing them to win the 1931 title without facing the second-place team?

    A. Chicago Bears
    B. Portsmouth Spartans
    C. New York Giants
    D. Frankford Yellow Jackets

4. Though the league decreased to ten teams because of the Depression, which team joined in the same season?

    A. Staten Island Stapletons
    B. Brooklyn Dodgers
    C. Cleveland Indians
    D. Chicago Cardinals

5. True or False: The Bears won the 1932 championship because ties did not count against their winning percentage.

6. True or False: The Bears defeated the Spartans in a playoff game to end the 1932 season, but the league counted the Spartans' loss in the standings, which dropped them to third place.

7. The Boston Braves changed their team name to what in 1933?

    A. Pirates
    B. Eagles
    C. Reds
    D. Redskins (Commanders)

8. In the first-ever NFL Championship game, the Bears defeated which team?

A. Brooklyn Dodgers
   B. Boston Redskins (Commanders)
   C. New York Giants
   D. Pittsburgh Pirates

9. True or False: The Bears went 13-0 before winning another NFL Championship in 1934.

10. True or False: The 1934 season was the first time that teams were not assessed a five-yard penalty for an incomplete pass.

11. The 1935 season was the last one, until 2022, that teams played a differing number of games. How many did most of them play that season?

    A. 12
    B. 13
    C. 14
    D. 15

12. Which team defeated the New York Giants to win the 1935 NFL Championship Game?

    A. Green Bay Packers
    B. Chicago Cardinals
    C. Chicago Bears
    D. Detroit Lions

13. True or False: The 1936 NFL Championship marked the first and only time a team declined home field advantage for the game.

14. True or False: The 1936 season also marked the first draft ever held by the league.

15. A Cleveland team joined the league in 1937. What was their name?

    A. Redskins (Commanders)
    B. Rams
    C. Tornadoes
    D. Cardinals

16. Which player led the league in passing during the 1937 season?

    A. Bernie Masterson
    B. Arnie Herber
    C. Bob Monnett

D. Sammy Baugh

17. True or False: Roughing the passer penalties were introduced in 1938, taking ten yards for offending teams.

18. True or False: Mel Hein, a center for the Giants, was named MVP in 1938.

CHAPTER 7 ANSWERS:

1. False. The Packers won, but it was the Giants who had more wins.
2. True. Their season-ending tie with the Portsmouth Spartans kept them ahead of the Giants in win percentage.
3. B. Portsmouth Spartans. It was a controversial ending, and rules were enacted to prevent similar actions.
4. C. Cleveland Indians. The team finished in eighth place that season.
5. True. Their 7-1-6 season was better than Green Bay's 10-3-1 season.
6. True. It allowed the Packers to finish second.
7. D. Redskins (Commanders). They would later move to Washington D.C.
8. C. New York Giants. Chicago won 23-21.
9. False. The Bears' undefeated season was ruined by the Giants in the 1934 Championship.
10. True. Passing was punished when the risk didn't pay off.
11. A. 12. A storm prevented some teams from playing their 12th game that year.
12. D. Detroit Lions. The Lions won the game 26-7.
13. True. The Boston Redskins (Commanders) agreed to a neutral site game due to poor ticket sales in Boston.
14. True. It ended arms races for new players entering the league.
15. B. Rams. They finished in last place during their debut season.
16. D. Sammy Baugh. He collected 1,127 yards for the Redskins (Commanders).
17. False. The penalty was 15 yards.
18. True. The trophy was named after Joe F. Carr.

Did You Know?

The first time an NFL game was broadcast on television was in October 22, 1939.

CHAPTER 8:

THE 1940S

1. True or False: The 1940 NFL Championship game was the most lopsided result in NFL history.

2. True or False: Pittsburgh changed their name from the Pirates to the Steelers in 1940.

3. The 1941 season saw who named the first Commissioner of the league?

    A. Elmer Layden
    B. Jim Thorpe
    C. Joseph Carr
    D. Carl Storck

4. The Bears had to defeat which team in the 1941 Western Division Playoff Game before advancing to the Championship Game?

    A. Detroit Lions
    B. Green Bay Packers
    C. Chicago Cardinals
    D. Cleveland Rams

5. True or False: Don Hutson was the MVP winner in 1942, following his strong season with the Packers.

6. True or False: The Redskins (Commanders) lost to the Bears once again in the 1942 Championship Game.

7. Because of World War II, which two teams merged and played as one squad during the 1943 season?

    A. Rams and Lions
    B. Eagles and Steelers
    C. Giants and Redskins (Commanders)
    D. Bears and Cardinals

8. The Giants played against which team for the league's last scoreless tie in history, back on November 7, 1943?

A. Chicago Bears
B. Green Bay Packers
C. Detroit Lions
D. Brooklyn Dodgers

9. True or False: The 1944 season is the most recent to feature two winless teams.

10. True or False: The 1944 season featured a rule change that no longer awarded a touchback when an offensive team committed pass interference in the opponent's endzone.

11. Which team defeated the Redskins (Commanders) to win the 1945 Championship?

    A. Lions
    B. Rams
    C. Packers
    D. Bears

12. Which player was awarded the MVP during the 1945 season?

    A. Bob Waterfield
    B. Sid Luckman
    C. Steve Van Buren
    D. Jim Benton

13. True or False: The 1946 season was the first to allow players to return punts and blocked field goals from inside their own endzone.

14. True or False: Bill Dudley led the league in rushing yards with 604 during the 1946 season.

15. The 1947 season was the first to disallow games to be played on which day of the week?

    A. Tuesday
    B. Wednesday
    C. Thursday
    D. Friday

16. The Chicago Cardinals defeated which team to win the 1947 NFL Championship?

    A. Washington Redskins (Commanders)
    B. Boston Yanks

C. Pittsburgh Steelers
D. Philadelphia Eagles

17. True or False: The 1948 season was one of the lowest scoring in league history.

18. True or False: The end of the 1949 season came with an announced merger between the NFL and the All-America Football Conference.

CHAPTER 8 ANSWERS:

1. True. The Bears beat the Redskins (Commanders) 73-0.
2. True. They finished 2-7-2 in their first campaign with the new name.
3. A. Elmer Layden. The other three served as leaders before Layden, but not with the Commissioner title.
4. B. Green Bay Packers. The Bears defeated them 33-14.
5. True. He was a wide receiver and led the league in receiving yards that year.
6. False. The Redskins (Commanders) beat the Bears, stopping them from a perfect season.
7. B. Eagles and Steelers. Fans called them the "Steagles."
8. C. Detroit Lions. It's been 80 years since the last scoreless tie.
9. True. Brooklyn and Chicago Cardinals/Pittsburgh Steelers did not win that season.
10. True. It used to result in a turnover.
11. B. Rams. They won 15-14.
12. A. Bob Waterfield. He led the Rams to the Championship.
13. True. It used to be an automatic touchback.
14. True. He was also named the league MVP for that year.
15. A. Tuesday. Scheduling and logistics involved many more challenges in this era of the game.
16. D. Philadelphia Eagles. The Cardinals won 28-21.
17. False. It was the highest scoring in history until 2013.
18. True. Three AAFC teams were set to join the league in 1950.

DID YOU KNOW?

Plastic helmets were briefly outlawed during the 1948 season but reintroduced one year later.

CHAPTER 9:
THE 1950S

1. Which team became the first to have all its games televised, beginning with the 1950 season?

   A. San Francisco 49ers
   B. Los Angeles Rams
   C. Cleveland Browns
   D. Washington Redskins (Commanders)

2. Which team survived the conference tiebreaker and won the 1950 NFL Championship?

   A. Chicago Bears
   B. Los Angeles Rams
   C. New York Giants
   D. Cleveland Browns

3. True or False: The 1951 season was the first to ban tackles, guards, and the center from catching or touching a forward pass.

4. True or False: The Los Angeles Rams lost the 1951 NFL Championship Game to the Cleveland Browns.

5. The 1952 season was the first to introduce which portion of the game?

   A. Coin toss
   B. Regular season overtime
   C. Untimed down
   D. Pregame anthem

6. The Lions defeated which team to win the 1952 Championship Game?

   A. Rams
   B. Packers
   C. Browns
   D. Eagles

7. True or False: The Browns finished the 1953 regular season 11-1 but lost in the NFL Championship Game.

8. True or False: Joe Perry rushed for over 1,000 yards for the 49ers during the 1953 season.

9. In their third straight NFL Championship Game, the Browns beat which team to win?

   A. Lions
   B. Bears
   C. 49ers
   D. Rams

10. Lou Groza was named Player of the Year by Sporting News in 1954. He was an offensive tackle, and he also played which position?

    A. Safety
    B. Linebacker
    C. Place kicker
    D. Punter

11. True or False: Otto Graham won the UPI MVP award in 1955, while the NEA MVP went to Harlon Hill.

12. True or False: Jim Finks threw for over 2,270 yards during the 1955 season.

13. The Chicago Bears were blown out in the 1956 NFL Championship Game by which team?

    A. New York Giants
    B. Chicago Cardinals
    C. Cleveland Browns
    D. Washington Redskins (Commanders)

14. The 1956 season was the first to prevent the grabbing of an opponent's facemask, but you could still do it to players in which position until 1962?

    A. Quarterback
    B. Tackles/Guards
    C. Ball carrier
    D. Center

15. True or False: The Lions won another NFL Championship in 1957.

16. True or False: Jim Brown, quarterback for the Browns, was named the MVP by the Associated Press.

17. Which team beat the Giants in the first NFL Championship to require overtime?

    A. Baltimore Colts
    B. Los Angeles Rams
    C. Chicago Bears
    D. San Francisco 49ers

18. The Green Bay Packers finished dead last in 1958, causing them to hire who as their head coach going into the 1959 season?

    A. Weeb Ewbank
    B. George Halas
    C. Buck Shaw
    D. Vince Lombardi

CHAPTER 9 ANSWERS:

1. Los Angeles Rams. The Redskins (Commanders) were the second team to do so.
2. D. Cleveland Browns. They beat the Giants and the Rams to win the championship.
3. True. It's a rule that has lasted to this day.
4. False. The Rams beat the Browns 24-17 to win.
5. B. Regular season overtime. Ties would no longer have such a big impact on the standings.
6. C. Browns. The Lions won 17-7.
7. True. They lost to the Lions again.
8. True. He led the league in that category.
9. A. Lions. Their revenge was sweet, with a 56-10 victory.
10. C. Place kicker. His contribution to the team was important in their championship run.
11. True. Graham was also named Player of the Year.
12. True. He collected 2,270 yards during the 1955 season.
13. A. New York Giants. The final score was 47-7.
14. C. Ball carrier. It seems odd today, but the rule only exempted the ball carrier until 1962.
15. True. They defeated the Browns 59-14.
16. False. Brown played fullback for the Browns.
17. A. Baltimore Colts. The game has been dubbed "The Greatest Game Ever Played."
18. D. Vince Lombardi. It marked the turnaround for the team.

Did You Know?

Johnny Unitas was named MVP of the league in 1959, and his team also won the NFL Championship.

CHAPTER 10:
THE 1960S

1. True or False: Vince Lombardi's only postseason loss as a head coach came against the Eagles in 1960.

2. True or False: The Browns won the inaugural "Playoff Bowl," a third-place game after the NFL Championship Game in 1960.

3. Which team joined the NFL in the 1961 season?

    A. Dallas Cowboys
    B. Minnesota Vikings
    C. Oakland Raiders
    D. Los Angeles Chargers

4. Which player was selected as the 1961 Rookie of the Year by the Associated Press?

    A. Mike Ditka
    B. Y.A. Tittle
    C. Paul Hornung
    D. Tommy McDonald

5. True or False: The Packers won a record-tying 14 games in the 1962 season, culminating in their second-straight NFL Championship.

6. True or False: Allie Sherman of the Pittsburgh Steelers was named Coach of the Year in 1962.

7. Which Green Bay Packer was suspended for the entire 1963 season for gambling on his own team's games?

    A. Jim Taylor
    B. Tom Moore
    C. Paul Hornung
    D. Bart Starr

8. Which team won the NFL Championship in 1963, defeating the Giants?

    A. Packers

B. Rams
C. Bears
D. Colts

9. True or False: The 1964 season saw rosters increase from 37 to 42 players.

10. True or False: The Colts were shut out in the 1964 NFL Championship.

11. Which team won the last NFL Championship, before the Super Bowl replaced it in 1966?

    A. Cleveland Browns
    B. Green Bay Packers
    C. Dallas Cowboys
    D. Baltimore Colts

12. Joe Namath chose to play for the AFL's New York Jets but was drafted by which NFL team?

    A. Cleveland Browns
    B. San Francisco 49ers
    C. Dallas Cowboys
    D. St. Louis Cardinals

13. True or False: The first Super Bowl was called the AFL-NFL World Championship Game.

14. True or False: The Redskins (Commanders) and Giants game in 1966 featured the highest combined score of any NFL game in history.

15. In 1967, the Packers beat which team in a game now known as the "Ice Bowl"?

    A. Dallas Cowboys
    B. Miami Dolphins
    C. Baltimore Colts
    D. Detroit Lions

16. The 1967 Offensive and Defensive Rookies of the Year both came from which team?

    A. Baltimore Colts
    B. Los Angeles Rams
    C. Detroit Lions
    D. San Francisco 49ers

17. True or False: The 1968 season marked the first time the NFL Champions were not crowned world champion.

18. True or False: The Vikings defeated the Chiefs to win Super Bowl IV.

CHAPTER 10 ANSWERS:

1. True. Lombardi's Packers were ready to dominate, despite the loss.
2. False. The Browns lost to the Lions by one point.
3. B. Minnesota Vikings. They picked the NFL over the AFL.
4. A. Mike Ditka. It was a strong start to a big NFL career.
5. True. They tied a mark set by the 1926 Frankford Yellow Jackets.
6. False. Sherman coached the New York Giants.
7. C. Paul Hornung. A Lions player was also suspended for the season.
8. C. Bears. They won the game 14-10.
9. False. Rosters only increased to 40 in 1964.
10. True. MVP Johnny Unitas couldn't help his team score.
11. B. Green Bay Packers. They beat the Browns 23-12.
12. D. St. Louis Cardinals. Namath was paid $427,000 for three years.
13. True. The merger between the two leagues was represented in the name.
14. True. They scored a combined 113 points.
15. A. Dallas Cowboys. It was technically the NFL Championship Game, sending the winner to the Super Bowl.
16. C. Detroit Lions. Mel Farr won as a running back, and Lem Barley won as a cornerback.
17. True. The NFL Champion Browns lost to the AFL Champion Jets.
18. False. The Chiefs defeated the Vikings.

Did You Know?

O.J. Simpson was selected first overall by the Buffalo Bills in the 1969 NFL/AFL Draft.

CHAPTER 11:
THE 1970S

1. True or False: The 1970 season was the first to feature two conferences instead of two leagues.

2. True or False: Four teams from the NFC joined the AFC to balance the two conferences.

3. Which team defeated the Miami Dolphins to win Super Bowl VI in 1971?

    A. Dallas Cowboys
    B. Los Angeles Rams
    C. Green Bay Packers
    D. San Francisco 49ers

4. Which team's coach, George Allen, was named Coach of the Year in 1971?

    A. Dolphins
    B. Redskins (Commanders)
    C. Lions
    D. Vikings

5. True or False: The 1972 Miami Dolphins are the only team in history with a perfect season.

6. True or False: The 1972 standings were the first time that ties counted as half of a win, and half of a loss.

7. In 1973, which player became the first ever to rush for 2,000 yards in a single season?

    A. Larry Brown
    B. Ron Johnson
    C. O.J. Simpson
    D. Larry Csonka

8. The Dolphins won another championship in 1973, defeating which team in the Super Bowl?

A. Dallas Cowboys
   B. Washington Redskins (Commanders)
   C. Los Angeles Rams
   D. Minnesota Vikings

9. True or False: The 1974 season was the first to feature an overtime period for regular season games.

10. True or False: The Steelers defeated the Los Angeles Rams to win Super Bowl IX.

11. Which quarterback was named MVP of the 1975 season?
    A. Ken Anderson
    B. Fran Tarkenton
    C. Roger Staubach
    D. Jim Hart

12. The Steelers repeated as Super Bowl Champions in 1975 when they beat which team?
    A. Dallas Cowboys
    B. Los Angeles Rams
    C. St. Louis Cardinals
    D. Minnesota Vikings

13. True or False: The league expanded to 29 teams in 1976.

14. True or False: The 1976 Raiders became the first original AFL team to win the Super Bowl since the merger.

15. The 1977 season saw teams average 17.2 points per game, the lowest since what year?
    A. 1942
    B. 1949
    C. 1954
    D. 1955

16. The Cowboys defeated which team in Super Bowl XII?
    A. Oakland Raiders
    B. Pittsburgh Steelers
    C. Baltimore Colts
    D. Denver Broncos

17. True or False: Terry Bradshaw led the league in 1978 with 28 passing touchdowns.

18. True or False: The 1979 Steelers became the first team to win back-to-back Super Bowls on two different occasions.

CHAPTER 11 ANSWERS:

1. True. The American Football Conference and National Football Conference were born.
2. False. Only three teams moved from the NFC to the AFC in 1970.
3. A. Dallas Cowboys. They won 24-3.
4. B. Redskins (Commanders). They reached the playoffs as a wild card but lost to the 49ers 24-20.
5. True. They also had two rushers with 1,000 yards each.
6. True. Ties used to be ignored in the standings.
7. C. O.J. Simpson. His dominant performance was once thought unthinkable.
8. D. Minnesota Vikings. The final score was 24-7.
9. True. The league wanted to further decrease the number of ties.
10. False. The Steelers defeated the Vikings 16-6.
11. B. Fran Tarkenton. He was second in passing yards that year but had a 64.2 completion percentage.
12. A. Dallas Cowboys. The final score was 21-17.
13. False. The league expanded to 28 teams that year.
14. True. They defeated the Vikings 32-14.
15. A. 1942. The league would change rules to end the "Dead Ball Era" of the 1970s.
16. D. Denver Broncos. The Cowboys won 27-10.
17. True. He led the Steelers to the Super Bowl that year, too.
18. True. The record would be matched later, but the Steelers were there first.

Did You Know?

The 1979 season was the first to ban players from leading with the crown of their helmet to make tackles.

CHAPTER 12:
THE 1980S

1. True or False: The Philadelphia Eagles became the first Wild Card team to win the Super Bowl in 1980.

2. True or False: The 1980 New Orleans Saints lost their first 14 games, matching a 1976 record.

3. Which team set five terrible defensive records in 1981?

    A. New England Patriots
    B. Baltimore Colts
    C. New Orleans Saints
    D. Los Angeles Rams

4. Which team defeated the Cincinnati Bengals to win Super Bowl XVI?

    A. San Francisco 49ers
    B. Dallas Cowboys
    C. Tampa Bay Buccaneers
    D. New York Giants

5. True or False: The 1982 season was shortened to eight games due to a players' strike.

6. True or False: The Redskins (Commanders) beat the Dolphins to win Super Bowl XVII.

7. Which quarterback was selected first overall by the Baltimore Colts in 1983?

    A. Billy Sims
    B. John Elway
    C. Vinny Testaverde
    D. Jim McMahon

8. The Raiders beat which team in Super Bowl XVIII?

    A. 49ers
    B. Lions
    C. Rams

D. Redskins (Commanders)
9. True or False: The Colts moved from Baltimore to Indianapolis in 1984.
10. True or False: The 1984 49ers became the first team to win 18 games in a season, including playoffs.
11. The Chicago Bears won Super Bowl XX by defeating which team?
    A. Miami Dolphins
    B. Cleveland Browns
    C. LA Raiders
    D. New England Patriots
12. Which player led all quarterbacks in passing yards during the 1985 season?
    A. Dan Marino
    B. John Elway
    C. Ken O'Brien
    D. Jim McMahon
13. True or False: The New York Giants won Super Bowl XXI by defeating the Denver Broncos.
14. True or False: The 1986 Cincinnati Bengals collected 5,490 yards on offense, more than any other team that year.
15. The Broncos reached the Super Bowl again in the 1987 season but lost to which team by 32 points?
    A. Minnesota Vikings
    B. Washington Redskins (Commanders)
    C. Chicago Bears
    D. San Francisco 49ers
16. Which player was named Offensive Player of the Year in 1987, though his team lost in the Divisional round?
    A. Eric Dickerson
    B. John Elway
    C. Jerry Rice
    D. Joe Montana
17. True or False: The Bengals had the top offense in 1988 but lost in the Super Bowl to San Francisco.

18. True or False: The 1989 league MVP was Joe Montana, and his team cruised to another Super Bowl.

CHAPTER 12 ANSWERS:

1. False. The Oakland Raiders were the first Wild Card team to win the Super Bowl, which they did in 1980.
2. True. They matched what the Buccaneers had accomplished four years earlier.
3. B. Baltimore Colts. They allowed 68 touchdowns that season.
4. A. San Francisco 49ers. They won the game 26-21.
5. False. The season was shortened to nine games.
6. True. They won 27-17.
7. B. John Elway. Dan Marino was also selected in the first round that year.
8. D. Redskins (Commanders). The final score was 38-9.
9. True. The team has remained in Indianapolis ever since.
10. True. The undefeated Dolphins from 1972 only played 17 games, including the Super Bowl.
11. D. New England Patriots. The final score was 46-10.
12. A. Dan Marino. He collected 4,137 yards through the air that year.
13. True. The final score was 39-20.
14. False. They had 6,490, which led the league.
15. B. Washington Redskins (Commanders). It was two straight Super Bowl disappointments for the Broncos.
16. C. Jerry Rice. The 49ers lost to the Vikings 36-24 that year, ending their playoff run.
17. True. They lost 20-16 but led the league in points, total yards, and rushing yards.
18. True. The 49ers led the league with 442 points scored, along with 6,268 total yards.

Did You Know?

Barry Sanders was named the Offensive Rookie of the Year in 1989.

CHAPTER 13:

THE 1990S

1. True or False: Derrick Thomas set the NFL record with seven sacks in one game, in November of 1990.

2. True or False: Jimmy Johnson was named Coach of the Year in 1990, for his work with the Dallas Cowboys.

3. Which player was named Super Bowl MVP after his team won Super Bowl XXVI?

    A. Gerald Riggs
    B. Don Beebe
    C. Thurman Thomas
    D. Mark Rypien

4. Which running back was named the league MVP and Offensive Player of the Year in 1991?

    A. Thurman Thomas
    B. Barry Sanders
    C. Emmitt Smith
    D. Rodney Hampton

5. True or False: Steve Young was named the league MVP in 1992, taking the helm in San Francisco from Joe Montana.

6. True or False: Troy Aikman was named Super Bowl MVP after the Cowboys demolished the Bills in Super Bowl XXVII.

7. In the 1993 draft, the New England Patriots selected which player first overall?

    A. Marvin Jones
    B. Drew Bledsoe
    C. Willie Roal
    D. Jerome Bettis

8. In the 1993 season, the play clock was reduced from 45 seconds to how many?

A. 40
   B. 35
   C. 30
   D. 25

9. True or False: 1994 was the first year the NFL implemented a salary cap.

10. True or False: John Carney led all scorers in 1994 with 135 points for the San Diego Chargers.

11. Which team scored the most points during the 1995 season but did not reach the Super Bowl?

    A. Dallas Cowboys
    B. Detroit Lions
    C. San Francisco 49ers
    D. Pittsburgh Steelers

12. Which team won Super Bowl XXX, defeating the Steelers?

    A. Packers
    B. Cowboys
    C. Eagles
    D. Falcons

13. True or False: The 1996 season was the first for the Baltimore Ravens.

14. True or False: Desmond Howard returned a kickoff 99 yards in Super Bowl XXXI

15. Which quarterback led the league in 1997 with 35 touchdown passes?

    A. Steve Young
    B. John Elway
    C. Jeff George
    D. Brett Favre

16. Favre and which player both earned MVP honors at the end of the 1997 season?

    A. Barry Sanders
    B. Troy Aikman
    C. Terrell Davis
    D. Cris Carter

17. True or False: Peyton Manning was drafted first overall by the Indianapolis Colts in 1998.

18. True or False: St. Louis' offense, "The Greatest Show on Turf," scored 23 points to defeat the Tennessee Titans in Super Bowl XXXIV.

CHAPTER 13 ANSWERS:

1. True. He also collected six in a 1998 game.
2. True. It helped that Emmitt Smith was named Offensive Rookie of the Year.
3. D. Mark Rypien. The quarterback helped the Redskins (Commanders) defeat the Bills.
4. A. Thurman Thomas. He had 1,563 rushing yards to lead the league.
5. True. He was also named Offensive Player of the Year that season.
6. True. Dallas won the game by 35 points.
7. B. Drew Bledsoe. He still holds the record with 70 pass attempts in one game.
8. A. 40. Speeding up the game is always good for spectators.
9. True. It would prevent rich teams from dominating the league.
10. True. He kicked 34 field goals that season.
11. C. San Francisco 49ers. They scored 457 points but lost to Green Bay in the Divisional round.
12. B. Cowboys. They won 27-17.
13. True. They finished the year 4-12.
14. True. It was arguably the defining moment of the game, which ended with a 35-21 score.
15. D. Brett Favre. His Packers reached the Super Bowl but were stopped by the Broncos.
16. A. Barry Sanders. He rushed for 2,053 yards that season.
17. True. He was on his way to a Hall of Fame career.
18. True. Kurt Warner was undrafted but led his team to victory.

Did You Know?

John Elway and Barry Sanders both retired during the summer of 1999.

CHAPTER 14:
THE 2000S

1. True or False: In the 2000 NFL Draft, Tom Brady was drafted with the first overall pick by the New England Patriots.

2. True or False: The Baltimore Ravens won Super Bowl XXXV with Defensive Player of the Year Ray Lewis at linebacker.

3. The New England Patriots won Super Bowl XXXVI by beating which team, who had the league MVP at quarterback?

    A. Philadelphia Eagles
    B. St. Louis Rams
    C. Chicago Bears
    D. Green Bay Packers

4. Which player was drafted first overall in the 2001 NFL Draft?

    A. LaDainian Tomlinson
    B. Richard Seymour
    C. Michael Vick
    D. Drew Brees

5. True or False: The Houston Texans joined the NFL in 2002, making each division equal, with five teams each.

6. True or False: Dexter Jackson, quarterback for the Tampa Bay Buccaneers, was named MVP of Super Bowl XXXVII.

7. New England won Super Bowl XXXVIII, defeating which team?

    A. Carolina Panthers
    B. Philadelphia Eagles
    C. Green Bay Packers
    D. St. Louis Rams

8. Which running back collected the most yards during the 2003 season?

    A. Deuce McAllister
    B. LaDainian Tomlinson
    C. Ahman Green

D. Jamal Lewis

9. True or False: Eli Manning was selected first overall by the New York Giants in 2004.

10. True or False: Daunte Culpepper led the league in 2004 with 4,717 passing yards.

11. The first NFL regular season game played outside of the United States took place where in October 2005?

   A. London, England
   B. Paris, France
   C. Mexico City, Mexico
   D. Toronto, Canada

12. Which Seattle player led the league in 2005 when it came to scoring?

   A. Chris Warren
   B. Shaun Alexander
   C. Curt Warner
   D. Marshawn Lynch

13. True or False: Devin Hester returned the opening kickoff 92 yards for a touchdown, giving the Bears an early lead in Super Bowl XLI.

14. True or False: Super Bowl XLI was only the second championship game in any of the major North American sports to feature two black head coaches.

15. Which player led the NFL in 2006 with 31 passing touchdowns?

   A. Tom Brady
   B. Drew Brees
   C. Vince Young
   D. Peyton Manning

16. Which player was drafted first in the 2007 NFL Draft?

   A. Calvin Johnson
   B. Joe Thomas
   C. Adrian Peterson
   D. JaMarcus Russell

17. True or False: The 2008 Detroit Lions were the first to go winless since 1982.

18. True or False: The 2009 Colts and Patriots started the season 13-0, the first time two teams have accomplished the feat in the same year.

CHAPTER 14 ANSWERS:

1. False. Tom Brady was selected 199th overall in the sixth round pick
2. True. They crushed the New York Giants 34-7.
3. B. St. Louis Rams. Tom Brady was named Super Bowl MVP in just his second season.
4. C. Michael Vick. The Falcons selected the quarterback who was strong with his arms and legs.
5. False. Each division has four teams.
6. False. Jackson played safety.
7. A. Carolina Panthers. They won 32-29, and Tom Brady won another MVP award.
8. D. Jamal Lewis. He had 2,066 yards that season.
9. False. Eli Manning was selected by the San Diego Chargers.
10. True. He collected those yards while playing with the Minnesota Vikings.
11. C. Mexico City, Mexico. The Cardinals beat the 49ers 31-14 in front of 103,467 spectators.
12. B. Shaun Alexander. He scored 168 points with 28 touchdowns.
13. True. However, the Colts would come back to win 29-17.
14. True. The other was the 1975 NBA Finals.
15. D. Peyton Manning. He also led the league with a 101.0 passer rating.
16. D. JaMarcus Russell. The quarterback went to the Raiders.
17. True. The 1982 season was shortened by a strike, too.
18. False. The Colts and Saints both reached 13-0 in 2009.

DID YOU KNOW?

The Detroit Lions drafted Matthew Stafford with the first overall pick in 2009.

CHAPTER 15:

THE 2010S

1. True or False: The 2010 Seahawks were the first team with a losing record to make the playoffs after a full-length season.

2. True or False: Aaron Rodgers was named the MVP for Super Bowl XLV.

3. Which player led the league in receiving yards for the 2011 season?

   A. Wes Welker
   B. Calvin Johnson
   C. Victor Cruz
   D. Larry Fitzgerald

4. The Patriots lost Super Bowl XLVI to which team (that had also beaten them a couple of years prior)?

   A. New Orleans Saints
   B. Atlanta Falcons
   C. Green Bay Packers
   D. New York Giants

5. True or False: Super Bowl XLVII marked the first time two brothers coached against each other.

6. True or False: Robert Griffin III became the first player in history to pass for more than 300 yards and two touchdowns without an interception in his first start.

7. Though Peyton Manning was league MVP in 2013, his Broncos lost to which team in Super Bowl XLVIII?

   A. San Francisco 49ers
   B. Carolina Panthers
   C. Seattle Seahawks
   D. New Orleans Saints

8. The Broncos became the first team in NFL history to have how many players score at least ten touchdowns in a season?

A. Four
   B. Five
   C. Six
   D. Seven
9. True or False: Malcolm Butler intercepted Tom Brady on the one-yard line to win Super Bowl XLIX for the Seahawks.
10. True or False: In the 2014 season, the NFL raised the goal post height from 25 to 30 feet.
11. During the 2015 season, three teams announced plans to move back to Los Angeles. Which were approved?
    A. Chargers
    B. Rams
    C. Raiders
    D. Rams and Chargers
12. Which of these players was drafted highest in the 2015 NFL Draft?
    A. Amari Cooper
    B. Todd Gurley
    C. Marcus Mariota
    D. Stefon Diggs
13. True or False: Super Bowl LI has come to be remembered as "27-3," because of New England's comeback victory.
14. True or False: Besides the comeback story, Super Bowl LI was also the first to be decided in overtime.
15. In 2017, which team became the second since the 16-game schedule to finish without a victory?
    A. Detroit Lions
    B. San Diego Chargers
    C. Los Angeles Rams
    D. Cleveland Browns
16. Which team defeated the Patriots in Super Bowl LII?
    A. Eagles
    B. Vikings
    C. Saints
    D. Falcons

17. True or False: Both the AFC and NFC Championship games in the 2018 season went to overtime.

18. True or False: The 2019 playoffs would be the last to include 12 teams.

CHAPTER 15 ANSWERS:

1. True. They were 7-9 that season, and they're also the only losing team to win a playoff game.
2. True. The Packers defeated the Steelers 31-25.
3. B. Calvin Johnson. He had 1,681 yards on the season.
4. D. New York Giants. Eli Manning defeated Tom Brady for a second time.
5. True. The Harbaugh brothers faced off for that Super Bowl championship.
6. True. It was a strong showing for the young quarterback.
7. C. Seattle Seahawks. The Legion of Boom defense did its job.
8. B. Five. Manning had plenty of targets to choose from during that season.
9. False. Butler made the interception for the Patriots, defeating the Seahawks.
10. False. The goal post was raised from 30 to 35 feet.
11. B. Rams. The league voted 30-2 in their favor but did not approve the other two teams.
12. C. Marcus Mariota. He was drafted second. The first pick was Jameis Winston.
13. False. The game is remembered as "28-3."
14. True. Every other Super Bowl reached a conclusion in regulation time.
15. D. Cleveland Browns. They joined the Lions on that list of poor teams.
16. A. Eagles. The final score was 41-33.
17. True. The Patriots beat the Chiefs, while the Rams beat the Saints.
18. True. 14 teams would be included beginning in 2020.

DID YOU KNOW?

Kyler Murray was the first-round pick in 2019, going to the Arizona Cardinals.

CHAPTER 16:

PRO BOWLS

1. True or False: The first All-Star Game took place in 1938.

2. True or False: The format of the modern Pro Bowl was adopted in 1960.

3. The Pro Bowl was held in Los Angeles for how many years to begin the tradition?

    A. 12
    B. 17
    C. 21
    D. 24

4. The first Pro Bowl to be held before the Super Bowl was in which year?

    A. 1977
    B. 1994
    C. 2001
    D. 2010

5. True or False: Otto Graham of the Cleveland Browns was named MVP of the 1950 Pro Bowl.

6. True or False: Tom Brady is the only player who has been selected to 15 Pro Bowls.

7. Who is the youngest quarterback to ever make a Pro Bowl team?

    A. Jameis Winston
    B. Lamar Jackson
    C. Robert Griffin III
    D. Cam Newton

8. Which kicker has more points in the Pro Bowl than any other player?

    A. Sebastian Janikowski
    B. Morten Andersen
    C. David Akers

D. Garo Yepremian

9. Which player has more touchdowns in the Pro Bowl than any other player?
   A. Brandon Marshall
   B. Calvin Johnson
   C. Larry Fitzgerald
   D. Rob Gronkowski

10. True or False: Tyler Huntley made the Pro Bowl during the 2022 season, despite only scoring two touchdowns during the regular season.

11. True or False: O.J. Simpson holds the Pro Bowl record with 29 rushing attempts in one game.

12. Which quarterback holds the Pro Bowl record for pass attempts, set in 2004?
   A. Tom Brady
   B. Peyton Manning
   C. Donovan McNabb
   D. Brett Favre

13. Which player set the record for longest run from scrimmage in a Pro Bowl back in 1995?
   A. Jerome Bettis
   B. Emmitt Smith
   C. Barry Sanders
   D. Marshall Faulk

14. True or False: Jim Hart threw five interceptions in one Pro Bowl, back in 1977.

15. True or False: Jeff Blake holds the record for longest passing play, throwing an 83-yard touchdown to Yancey Thigpen in 1996.

16. Only one player has scored three touchdowns in one Pro Bowl. Who did it, in 2000?
   A. Randy Moss
   B. Mike Alstott
   C. Tony Gonzalez
   D. Jimmy Smith

17. Which receiver had ten catches in the 2013 Pro Bowl, a record?
    A. Victor Cruz
    B. Calvin Johnson
    C. Reggie Wayne
    D. Demaryius Thomas
18. True or False: Walter Payton has more career yards of offense than any other Pro Bowl player.

CHAPTER 16 ANSWERS:

1. True. The first All-Star Game was played in 1939 to benefit the Salvation Army.
2. False. The format was adopted in 1950, pitting players from each conference against each other.
3. C. 21. After those first 21 years, the game bounced around, much like the Super Bowl, for almost a decade.
4. D. 2010. It was also held in the same stadium as the Super Bowl, and it led to poor ratings.
5. True. It was a 28-27 victory for the American Conference.
6. True. Four players have 14 selections, but Brady is alone at the top with 15.
7. A. Jameis Winston. He is the only quarterback to earn a selection before turning 22.
8. C. David Akers. He's collected 57 points in six Pro Bowl games.
9. C. Larry Fitzgerald. He has eight touchdowns in seven Pro Bowl games.
10. True. It's the fewest TDs for any Pro Bowl selection.
11. False. He holds the record, but it's only 19 attempts during the 1974 Pro Bowl.
12. B. Peyton Manning. He threw the ball 41 times that game.
13. D. Marshall Faulk. He had a 49-yard run during that game.
14. True. It is the record for most INTs in a single Pro Bowl game.
15. False. The pass was 93 yards.
16. B. Mike Alstott. He had three TD runs totaling five yards of offense.
17. A. Victor Cruz. Only one of those catches was for a touchdown.
18. True. He collected 368 yards in nine Pro Bowls.

Did You Know?

Only three safeties have occurred in Pro Bowls. 1983, 1985, and 1992.

CHAPTER 17:
THE AMERICAN FOOTBALL CONFERENCE

1. True or False: The AFC was founded in 1970, ten years after the NFL merged with the AFL.

2. True or False: The AFC Champion is presented with the George S. Halas trophy.

3. Which of these teams did not leave the NFL to join the AFC when the merger happened in 1970?

    A. Baltimore Colts
    B. Cleveland Browns
    C. Pittsburgh Steelers
    D. St. Louis Cardinals

4. In 1976, which team joined the AFC?

    A. Denver Broncos
    B. Kansas City Chiefs
    C. Tampa Bay Buccaneers
    D. Buffalo Bills

5. True or False: The Seahawks and Buccaneers switched conferences in 1977, sending Seattle to the AFC.

6. True or False: In 1995, the Carolina Panthers joined the AFC.

7. Which AFC Central team got a new home and new name in 1996?

    A. Cleveland Browns
    B. Cincinnati Bengals
    C. Pittsburgh Steelers
    D. Houston Oilers

8. Which team joined the AFC in 2002?

    A. Oakland Raiders
    B. Houston Texans

C. Cleveland Browns
D. Jacksonville Jaguars

9. True or False: The Houston Texans are the only AFC team yet to reach the AFC Championship Game.

10. True or False: The Steelers have the most AFC Championship appearances, with 16.

11. Which team has won the most AFC Championships?
    A. Kansas City Chiefs
    B. Pittsburgh Steelers
    C. New England Patriots
    D. Denver Broncos

12. Which AFC team holds the record by hosting the AFC Championship five years in a row?
    A. Kansas City Chiefs
    B. Pittsburgh Steelers
    C. New England Patriots
    D. Denver Broncos

13. True or False: The Broncos and Steelers have reached an AFC Championship every decade.

14. True or False: The Patriots hold the record for playing in the most consecutive AFC Championship games, with eight.

15. Which AFC Champion scored the most points in the AFC Championship Game?
    A. Miami Dolphins
    B. Buffalo Bills
    C. New England Patriots
    D. Oakland Raiders

16. In what year was the last time an AFC Championship Game ended in a shutout?
    A. 1971
    B. 1982
    C. 1991
    D. 2001

17. True or False: The 1987 Browns hold the distinction of scoring the most points in an AFC Championship Game by a losing team.

18. True or False: The Buffalo Bills hold the record for most consecutive AFC Championship wins.

CHAPTER 17 ANSWERS:

1. True. The AFL began in 1960 and added two more teams before the full merger.
2. False. The AFC Championship trophy is named after Lamar Hunt.
3. D. St. Louis Cardinals. The other three teams moved to the new AFC to help balance the conferences.
4. C. Tampa Bay Buccaneers. They joined the AFC West, leaving only the Central with four teams.
5. True. The Seahawks went to the AFC West.
6. False. The Jacksonville Jaguars joined the AFC while the Panthers joined the NFC.
7. A. Cleveland Browns. They became the Baltimore Ravens.
8. B. Houston Texans. They joined the AFC South.
9. True. Every other team has reached the AFC Championship Game.
10. True. Of those games, 11 were in Pittsburgh, the most conference championships hosted by any team.
11. C. New England Patriots. They have 11 titles.
12. A. Kansas City Chiefs. They hosted the title game from 2018 to 2022.
13. True. No other team has accomplished that feat.
14. True. They were in the game from 2011 to 2018.
15. B. Buffalo Bills. They scored 51 points against the LA Raiders in 1990.
16. B. 1982. The Dolphins shut out the Jets.
17. False. The 2006 Patriots scored 34 points and lost. The 1987 Browns scored 33.
18. True, they won four from 1990 to 1993. It's the most for either conference.

Did You Know?

The 1991 Buffalo Bills only scored ten points in the AFC Championship Game, but they still won.

CHAPTER 18:
THE NATIONAL FOOTBALL CONFERENCE

1. True or False: The NFC's original divisional alignment was determined by selecting one plan, out of five, from a glass bowl.

2. True or False: The original NFC logo was in use from 1970 until 2011.

3. How many stars graced the "N" of the NFC's original logo?

   A. Zero
   B. One
   C. Two
   D. Three

4. Which was the first team to join the NFC after its creation in 1970?

   A. Washington Redskins (Commanders)
   B. Seattle Seahawks
   C. Minnesota Vikings
   D. New Orleans Saints

5. True or False: The Seahawks only spent one year in the NFC.

6. True or False: The Carolina Panthers joined the NFC in 1995.

7. Which team switched from the AFC West to the NFC West in 2002?

   A. Denver Broncos
   B. Oakland Raiders
   C. Seattle Seahawks
   D. Arizona Cardinals

8. The NFC Championship trophy is named after which figure from football history?

   A. Bert Bell
   B. George Halas
   C. Red Grange
   D. John McNally

9. True or False: Every NFC team has reached the NFC Championship at least once.

10. True or False: The Detroit Lions are the only NFC team to never win the NFC Championship.

11. Which of these teams has never defeated the Dallas Cowboys in the NFC Championship?

    A. Chicago Bears
    B. San Francisco 49ers
    C. Washington Redskins (Commanders)
    D. Minnesota Vikings

12. Which team scored the most points in the NFC Championship Game, as of 2023?

    A. Atlanta Falcons
    B. Carolina Panthers
    C. Washington Redskins (Commanders)
    D. New York Giants

13. True or False: The largest margin of victory in an NFC Championship game is 41 points.

14. True or False: As of 2023, the last team to repeat as NFC Champions is the San Francisco 49ers.

15. Which team has reached the NFC Championship more than any other team?

    A. Dallas Cowboys
    B. Green Bay Packers
    C. San Francisco 49ers
    D. Los Angeles Rams

16. The 49ers are tied with which team for the most NFC Championship wins?

    A. Dallas Cowboys
    B. Green Bay Packers
    C. Los Angeles Rams
    D. Minnesota Vikings

17. True or False: The New York Giants are 5-0 in NFC Championship games.

18. True or False: The Washington Redskins (Commanders) have won every NFC Championship game they have hosted.

CHAPTER 18 ANSWERS:

1. True. The NFL commissioner's secretary had the honor of pulling the selected plan from the bowl.
2. False. The original NFC logo was retired in 2009.
3. D. Three. The three stars run along the angled middle line of the N.
4. B. Seattle Seahawks. The Buccaneers also joined the AFC at the same time.
5. True. After one year, they switched conferences with the Buccaneers.
6. True. It was their first season in the league.
7. C. Seattle Seahawks. They had been in the AFC from 1977 to 2001.
8. B. George Halas. He was the founder of the Chicago Bears, among other contributions.
9. True. Though, there is only one team that has never won it.
10. True. They are 0-2 as of 2023.
11. A. Chicago Bears. Every other team listed has a victory against the Cowboys in the NFC Championship.
12. B. Carolina Panthers. They scored 49 points against the Cardinals in 2015-16.
13. True. The 2000-01 Giants defeated the Vikings 41-0.
14. False. The last team to repeat as NFC Champions was the Seahawks.
15. C. San Francisco 49ers. They have reached 19 times.
16. A. Dallas Cowboys. They have eight wins in only 14 appearances.
17. True. They've allowed an average of ten points in those contests.
18. True. They are 5-0 at home, 0-1 on the road.

DID YOU KNOW?

Teams from the NFC West have the most appearances in the NFC Championship, with 37.

CHAPTER 19:

AFC EAST

1. Which Buffalo Bills quarterback has more passing yards for the franchise than any other player?

   A. Joe Ferguson
   B. Josh Allen
   C. Jim Kelly
   D. Jack Kemp

2. In Bills history, which player leads the organization in all-time rushing yards?

   A. Thurman Thomas
   B. O.J. Simpson
   C. Fred Jackson
   D. Joe Cribbs

3. True or False: As of 2023, Andre Reed has the most receiving yards as any other Bills player in team history.

4. True or False: Ryan Lindell leads the Bills in all-time points scored.

5. Which Miami Dolphins quarterback has more passing yards and touchdowns than any other Dolphin?

   A. Bob Griese
   B. Dan Marino
   C. Ryan Tannehill
   D. Tua Tagovailoa

6. Which Dolphins fullback leads the organization in rushing yards and rushing touchdowns?

   A. Ricky Williams
   B. Ronnie Brown
   C. Karim Abdul-Jabbar
   D. Larry Csonka

7. True or False: Mark Clayton has more receiving yards than any other Miami player in team history.

8. True or False: Garo Yepremian leads the Dolphins organization in scoring.

9. Tom Brady leads the New England Patriots in all-time passing yards, but who is second?

    A. Steve Grogan
    B. Drew Bledsoe
    C. Babe Parilli
    D. Tony Eason

10. Which New England Patriot has the most rushing yards but not the most rushing touchdowns?

    A. Jim Nance
    B. Tony Collins
    C. Curtis Martin
    D. Sam Cunningham

11. True or False: Rob Gronkowski leads the Patriots in all-time receiving yards.

12. True or False: Stephen Gostkowski leads all Patriots in points.

13. Which quarterback leads all New York Jets in passing yards and touchdowns?

    A. Joe Namath
    B. Ken O'Brien
    C. Richard Todd
    D. Chad Pennington

14. As of 2023, only one Jet has run for more than 10,000 yards with the team. Who?

    A. Freeman McNeil
    B. Curtis Martin
    C. Emerson Boozer
    D. Matt Snell

15. True or False: Don Maynard is the only receiver from the Jets with more than 10,000 receiving yards with the team.

16. True or False: Nick Folk is the Jets all-time leading scorer.

17. Of the four current AFC East teams, which one has the fewest division titles?

    A. New England Patriots
    B. Buffalo Bills
    C. Miami Dolphins
    D. New York Jets

18. Which AFC East team has the most Wild Card playoff berths?

    A. New York Jets
    B. Buffalo Bills
    C. Miami Dolphins
    D. New England Patriots

CHAPTER 19 ANSWERS:

1. C. Jim Kelly. He played 160 games with the team from 1986 to 1996. It was a solid career considering Kelly spent his first two years of professional football with the USFL's Houston Gamblers. He was selected by the Bills 14th overall but chose to join the Gamblers. He is also well known for one game in 1985 when he threw for 574 yards in a 34-33 victory over a Los Angeles Express team led by Steve Young.
2. A. Thurman Thomas. He rushed for 11,938 yards from 1988 to 1999. He won a league MVP in 1991 for his skills as a running back, and he also received five Pro Bowl nominations, all in the first half of his career. When he retired from the league, he held a rushing average of 4.2 yards per carry, an impressive number for any running back.
3. True. He had 13,095 yards when he played from 1985 to 1999. In his 15 seasons with the Bills, Reed was selected to the Pro Bowl seven times, and he still ranks in the top ten when it comes to receptions in the playoffs, with 85.
4. False. Kicker Steve Christie leads the Bills with 1,011 career points. Christie was well known for his ability to kick accurately even when poor weather would hamper the abilities of other kickers around the league. He kicked a 59-yard field goal in 1993, which was only four yards short of the NFL record at the time. He is still tied for most field goals made in overtime periods, with nine.
5. B. Dan Marino. He had 61,361 yards and 420 touchdown passes in his 17 seasons with the Dolphins. He was the first quarterback in the history of the NFL to pass for more than 5,000 yards in a season, and although he never won a Super Bowl during his playing career, many still consider him to be one of the best quarterbacks of all time.
6. D. Larry Csonka. He had 6,737 yards and 53 rushing touchdowns during his time with the Dolphins. He was the first overall pick by the Dolphins in the 1968 Common Draft, and his impact on the team was so immense that he is one of only three players to have their number retired by the team. Of course, he also played a major role in the Dolphins' perfect season, an unmatched feat to this day.
7. False. Mark Duper has 8,869 yards, and Clayton has 8,643. Duper played 11 seasons with the Dolphins, three of which included Pro Bowl selections. Along with his yards, Duper collected 59 touchdowns on 511 catches during his career. Though he did not

reach the Hall of Fame, he was inducted into the Miami Dolphins Honor Roll in 2003.
8. False. Olindo Mare leads the organization with 1,048 points. His career was particularly impressive considering he was an undrafted free agent in 1996 and cut by the Giants before finding his way to the Dolphins. He spent the next ten seasons with the team, becoming their all-time leading scorer along the way. At the end of his career, Mare had an 81.1% field goal success rate.
9. B. Drew Bledsoe. Brady had 74,571 yards to Bledsoe's 29,657. Though Bledsoe's career is often an afterthought compared to Brady, it needs to be remembered that Bledsoe helped the Patriots rebuild. He even played in the 2001 AFC Championship when Brady was injured. He was inducted into the Patriots Hall of Fame for his efforts.
10. D. Sam Cunningham. He had 5,453 yards, only 130 more than Nance. During his ten years with the Patriots, he also collected 1,905 receiving yards and a total of 49 touchdowns. While the team struggled during those years, Cunningham was one of the bright spots.
11. False. Stanley Morgan leads the Patriots in all-time receiving yards. It helps that he holds the NFL record for yards per catch, 19.2. If Morgan caught the ball, it was an almost-guaranteed long-yardage play.
12. True. He scored 1,775 points playing from 2006 to 2019. He was selected to four Pro Bowls and won three Super Bowls during his time with the Patriots. He also led the NFL in scoring for five seasons.
13. A. Joe Namath. He threw for 27,057 yards from 1965 to 1976. Namath won Super Bowl III and was named to the Pro Bowl in 1972.
14. B. Curtis Martin. He played as a member of the Jets from 1998 to 2005, though he also spent three seasons with the Patriots. He was a five-time Pro Bowler and averaged 4.0 yards per carry over his career.
15. True. He had 11,732 yards when he played from 1960 to 1972. Over the course of his career, he caught 88 touchdown passes. His number, 13, was retired by the Jets.
16. False. Pat Leahy leads the Jets in all-time points with 1,470. He joined the team as a free agent after their starting kicker suffered a leg injury. However, he kept the position and went on to complete 71.4% of his field goal attempts and more than 95% of his point-after attempts. He's in the top 30 of all scorers in NFL history.
17. D. New York Jets. They only have four division titles.

18. A. New York Jets. As of 2023, they have ten Wild Card berths.

Did You Know?

From 2001 to 2018, the New England Patriots won six Super Bowls.

CHAPTER 20:

AFC NORTH

1. True or False: As of 2023, Lamar Jackson is the Ravens' all-time leading passer.

2. True or False: Jamal Lewis is the Ravens' all-time leading rusher.

3. Which Ravens receiver leads the organization with 5,777 receiving yards?

    A. Todd Heap
    B. Mark Andrews
    C. Torrey Smith
    D. Derrick Mason

4. Two Ravens have more than 1,000 points. Who has the most?

    A. Matt Stover
    B. Justin Tucker
    C. Billy Cundiff
    D. Jamal Lewis

5. True or False: Two Bengals quarterbacks have gathered more than 30,000 passing yards.

6. True or False: As of 2023, Corey Dillon leads the Bengals in all-time rush yards.

7. Only one Bengals receiver has more than 10,000 receiving yards. Who is it?

    A. A.J. Green
    B. Isaac Curtis
    C. Chad Johnson
    D. Carl Pickens

8. Only one Bengals player has scored more than 1,000 points. Who is it?

    A. Shayne Graham
    B. Mike Nugent

C. Jim Breech
D. Doug Pelfrey

9. True or False: Brian Sipe leads the Browns in all-time passing yards.

10. True or False: Leroy Kelly is the only rusher with more than 10,000 yards with the Browns.

11. Which Browns receiver has 7,980 receiving yards, more than any other player in the organization?

    A. Ozzie Newsome
    B. Dante Lavelli
    C. Mac Speedie
    D. Ray Renfro

12. Which Browns kicker had 1,608 points, playing over 20 years with the team?

    A. Phil Dawson
    B. Don Cockroft
    C. Jim Brown
    D. Lou Groza

13. True or False: Terry Bradshaw leads the Steelers in all-time passing yards.

14. True or False: Franco Harris has more rushing yards than any other Steelers player in history.

15. Two Steelers have more than 10,000 receiving yards, but which player has the most?

    A. Antonio Brown
    B. John Stallworth
    C. Hines Ward
    D. Heath Miller

16. Which kicker is the only Steeler to score more than 1,000 points for the organization?

    A. Chris Boswell
    B. Gary Anderson
    C. Jeff Reed
    D. Roy Gerela

17. True or False: The Steelers have twice as many division titles compared to any other team in their division.

18. True or False: The Cleveland Browns have six division titles but zero AFC titles.

CHAPTER 20 ANSWERS:

1. False. Joe Flacco leads the Ravens in all-time passing with 38,245 yards in the air. Besides being known for having one of the strongest arms in the history of the league, Joe Flacco has the most passing yards and touchdowns by any quarterback who has never participated in a Pro Bowl game. He was invited to one but declined to participate.
2. True. His 7,801 rushing yards is good enough to be top of the list in the organization. He was the fifth overall pick in 2000, and he helped the Ravens to a victory in Super Bowl XXXV. By the end of his career, he surpassed 10,000 rushing yards and 58 rushing touchdowns.
3. D. Derrick Mason. He played 96 games with the team from 2005 to 2010. Before he joined the Ravens, he was named to two Pro Bowls as a member of the Tennessee Oilers/Titans. By the end of his career, he had 12,061 receiving yards and 66 touchdown catches.
4. B. Justin Tucker. As of 2023, he has 1,649 points with the Ravens. As of 2023, he has played 12 seasons with the Ravens, and his career field goal percentage sits at 90.2%. If that number holds for the rest of his career, he will hold the NFL record in that statistic.
5. True. Ken Anderson and Andy Dalton have both reached the milestone with the team.
6. True. He rushed for 8,061 yards from 1997 to 2003. In those seven seasons, he was named to three Pro Bowls before moving to the Patriots in 2004. He was a member of the Super Bowl XXXIX championship team, and New England also named him to their All-Dynasty Team.
7. C. Chad Johnson. He had 10,783 yards from 2001 to 2010. He played a couple more seasons for other teams, but he struggled to maintain his performance levels. He was a six-time Pro Bowler, and he received Ring of Honor awards from the Cincinnati Bengals.
8. C. Jim Breech. He had 1,151 points from 1980 to 1992. He played one season with the Raiders, too, before heading to the Bengals. He played in two Super Bowls and did not miss a field goal in either contest, though his team did not win. He was also known for wearing two different sizes of cleats. He preferred a smaller cleat on his kicking foot.

9. True. He had 23,713 yards from 1974–1983, and he was even named NFL MVP in 1980. While he led the league in passing touchdowns in 1979, it was that 1980 season that cemented his place in Browns history.
10. False. Jim Brown is the only rusher to reach that milestone. Brown played for the Browns from 1957 to 1965, and during those years, he won three league MVP awards, nine Pro Bowls, and one NFL championship. He also led the league in rushing for eight seasons, and he even led the league in scoring for one year.
11. A. Ozzie Newsome. He played from 1978 to 1990 as a tight end. He was a Pro Bowl selection three times, and he was also named First-team All-Pro twice during his career.
12. D. Lou Groza. He played from 1946 to 1967. His career was notable as he played both offensive tackle and placekicker. Thanks to Groza's last-minute field goal, the Browns won the NFL Championship in their first season of existence. His kicking was so good that he was nicknamed "The Toe."
13. False. Ben Roethlisberger leads the Steelers in all-time passing yards with 64,088. "Big Ben" played for the Steelers for his entire career, which spanned 18 seasons, two Super Bowl victories, six Pro Bowls, and he led the league in passing yards twice.
14. True. His 11,950 yards are the most in the franchise. He played 12 seasons with the Steelers during a period of dominance for the team. He helped the team win four Super Bowl championships, and he earned one Super Bowl MVP. Of those 12 seasons, he was selected to the Pro Bowl nine times, as well.
15. C. Hines Ward. He collected 12,083 yards from 1998 to 2011. His entire career was spent with the Steelers, so he also leads the team in receptions and touchdown catches. He also won two Super Bowls with the team, and he earned Super Bowl MVP for one of those victories.
16. B. Gary Anderson. He scored 1,343 points from 1982 to 1994. His entire career was longer, as he continued playing until 2004, collecting four Pro Bowl selections and one league scoring title.
17. True. As of 2023, they have captured 24 division titles.
18. True. They have never reached the Super Bowl.

Did You Know?

Only the Steelers and Ravens have won Super Bowl titles as representatives of the AFC North.

CHAPTER 21:

AFC SOUTH

1. True or False: Deshaun Watson has more passing yards than any other Houston Texans player.

2. True or False: Arian Foster leads the Texans in all-time rushing yards.

3. Which Texans receiver has the most touchdowns for the organization?

    A. DeAndre Hopkins
    B. Andre Johnson
    C. Owen Daniels
    D. Kevin Walter

4. As of 2023, which player has the most points in Texans history?

    A. Kris Brown
    B. Arian Foster
    C. Ka'imi Fairbairn
    D. Andre Johnson

5. True or False: Peyton Manning had a better pass completion percentage over his career with the Colts than Andrew Luck did.

6. True or False: Edgerrin James is the only Colt with more than 10,000 rushing yards.

7. Four Colts have more than 9,000 receiving yards. Who has the most?

    A. Reggie Wayne
    B. T.Y. Hilton
    C. Raymond Berry
    D. Marvin Harrison

8. Which kicker leads all Colts in career scoring?

    A. Mike Vanderjagt
    B. Dean Biasucci
    C. Adam Vinatieri
    D. Lou Michaels

9. True or False: Blake Bortles leads the Jaguars in all-time touchdowns thrown.

10. True or False: Fred Taylor leads all Jaguars in rushing yards.

11. Only one Jaguar has more than 10,000 receiving yards. Who is it?
    A. Jimmy Smith
    B. Keegan McCardell
    C. Marcedes Lewis
    D. Maurice Jones-Drew

12. Which Jaguars defender has more interceptions for the team than any other?
    A. Aaron Beasley
    B. Donovin Darius
    C. Derek Cox
    D. Rashean Mathis

13. True or False: Warren Moon and George Blanda lead the Titans in all-time passing yards.

14. True or False: The only Titan with more than 10,000 rushing yards is Derrick Henry.

15. The Titans' leading rusher is which player, who played from 1986 to 1994?
    A. Drew Hill
    B. Ken Burrough
    C. Ernest Givins
    D. Charley Hennigan

16. Which kicker leads all Titans in scoring, and his last season was in 2000?
    A. Rob Bironas
    B. George Blanda
    C. Tony Zendejas
    D. Al Del Greco

17. True or False: Teams from the AFC South have accounted for two Super Bowl victories.

18. True or False: The Houston Texans are the only AFC South team to never reach the AFC Championship Game, as of 2023.

CHAPTER 21 ANSWERS:

1. False. Matt Schaub is the Texans' leading passer, with 23,221 yards. Schaub played for a total of 17 seasons, but only seven of those were with the Texans. He was selected for two Pro Bowls while with the team.
2. True. He had 6,472 yards from 2009 to 2015, which also included four Pro Bowl selections. He led the NFL in rushing touchdowns twice and led the league once in rushing yards.
3. B. Andre Johnson. He caught 64 touchdowns from 2003 to 2014.
4. A. Kris Brown. He had 767 points from 2002 to 2009. He is the only kicker to make three field goals from 54 yards or further in a single game.
5. True. He had a 64.9% completion rate, and Luck's was 60.8%.
6. False. James leads all Colts in rushing yards, but he only has 9,226 yards.
7. D. Marvin Harrison. He had 14,580 yards during his career, which he spent entirely with the Colts. He helped the team win one Super Bowl, and he was selected to eight Pro Bowls.
8. C. Adam Vinatieri. He scored 1,515 points from 2006 to 2019.
9. False. Mark Brunell has 144 touchdown passes to Bortles' 103.
10. True. He had 11,271 yards from 1998 to 2008.
11. A. Jimmy Smith. He had 12,287 yards from 1995 to 2005. During that time, Smith won two Super Bowls and earned five Pro Bowl selections. He led the league in catches during the 1999 season.
12. D. Rashean Mathis. He collected 30 interceptions from 2003 to 2012. His performance with the Jaguars led to one First-team All-Pro selection and one Pro Bowl selection.
13. False. Moon and Steve McNair lead in passing yards, but Blanda is in second place when it comes to touchdown passes.
14. False. Eddie George is the only Titan to surpass 10,000 rushing yards. He played all but one year of his career with the Oilers/Titans, which included four Pro Bowl selections.
15. C. Ernest Givins. He got 7,935 yards during his time with the team.
16. D. Al Del Greco. He scored 1,060 points while playing from 1991 to 2000. Impressively, Del Greco made 99.46% of his career extra-point attempts.

17. False. Only the 2006 Colts have won a Super Bowl from the AFC South.
18. True. Every other team has reached the AFC Championship.

DID YOU KNOW?

The Jacksonville Jaguars have only reached the playoffs four times in the history of the AFC South.

CHAPTER 22:

AFC WEST

1. True or False: John Elway has more passing yards than any other Broncos passer.

2. True or False: Terrell Davis had 7,607 rushing yards for the Broncos, the most in team history.

3. Only one Broncos receiver has surpassed 10,000 receiving yards. Who is it?

   A. Demaryius Thomas
   B. Shannon Sharpe
   C. Rod Smith
   D. Lionel Taylor

4. Which kicker has scored more points than any other Broncos player?

   A. Brandon McManus
   B. Jason Elam
   C. Jim Turner
   D. Matt Prater

5. True or False: As of 2023, Len Dawson leads the Kansas City Chiefs in passing yards and touchdowns.

6. True or False: Priest Holmes leads all Kansas City players in rushing touchdowns.

7. Which Chiefs receiver leads the organization in receiving yards?

   A. Tony Gonzalez
   B. Otis Taylor
   C. Travis Kelce
   D. Dwayne Bowe

8. As of 2023, which kicker leads all Chiefs in points scored?

   A. Nick Lowery
   B. Jan Stenerud
   C. Harrison Butker

D. Ryan Succop

9. True or False: Derek Carr leads all Raiders with 217 touchdown passes.

10. True or False: The Raiders' leading rusher is Marcus Allen, who played in the 1980s.

11. Only one Raider has surpassed 10,000 receiving yards, as of 2023. Who is it?
    A. Fred Biletnikoff
    B. Cliff Branch
    C. Tim Brown
    D. Todd Christensen

12. Which player has more points than any other Raider?
    A. Sebastian Janikowski
    B. George Blanda
    C. Chris Bahr
    D. Daniel Carlson

13. True or False: Philip Rivers threw for 397 touchdowns with the Chargers.

14. True or False: LaDainian Tomlinson leads all Chargers in rushing yards.

15. As of 2023, which Chargers player has more receiving yards than any other player?
    A. Keenan Allen
    B. Lance Alworth
    C. Charlie Joiner
    D. Antonio Gates

16. Which player has more points for the Chargers than any other player?
    A. Nate Kaeding
    B. Rolf Benirschke
    C. John Carney
    D. LaDainian Tomlinson

17. True or False: Since 1960, the AFC West has sent 20 teams to the Super Bowl.

18. True or False: The Chargers have the fewest playoff berths of the current AFC West teams.

CHAPTER 22 ANSWERS:

1. True. Peyton Manning is in second, though Elway leads him by more than 30,000 yards. John Elway spent his entire 16-year career with the Broncos, winning two Super Bowls, one Super Bowl MVP, one league MVP, and nine Pro Bowls. He is widely considered one of the top quarterbacks of all time.
2. True. The next closest player is Floyd Little.
3. C. Rod Smith. He had 11,389 yards from 1995 to 2006. He won two Super Bowls with the Broncos, along with three Pro Bowl selections. He led the league in receptions during the 2001 season as well. He was inducted into the Broncos Ring of Fame for his contributions to the team.
4. B. Jason Elam. He scored 1,786 points from 1993 to 2007.
5. True. Patrick Mahomes is likely to pass him during the 2024 season.
6. True. He collected 76 touchdowns from 2001 to 2007. Holmes won Offensive Player of the Year in his second year with the Chiefs, when he also led the league in scoring and rushing touchdowns. He had three Pro Bowl selections that all came with the Chiefs, though he was part of the 2000 Ravens, who won the Super Bowl.
7. C. Travis Kelce. He had 11,328 yards as of 2023.
8. A. Nick Lowery. He scored 1,466 points from 1980 to 1993.
9. True. Carr also leads in passing yards, with 35,222. Carr played nine seasons with the Raiders before heading to the New Orleans Saints. During his time with the Raiders, Carr collected four Pro Bowl selections. As of 2023, his passer rating is 92.3.
10. True. He collected 8,545 yards from 1982 to 1992.
11. C. Tim Brown. He had 14,734 yards from 1988 to 2003. During his time with the Raiders, he set the NFL record for consecutive starts by a receiver with 176, and he was selected to nine Pro Bowls.
12. A. Sebastian Janikowski. He scored 1,799 points from 2000 to 2017, which included a Pro Bowl selection. His career field goal percentage was 80.4%, and his longest was a 63-yard kick.
13. True. He also collected 59,271 passing yards.
14. True. He had 12,490 yards. Paul Lowe was in second place with 4,972 yards.

15. D. Antonio Gates. His 11,841 yards is 1,300 more than Keenan Allen, as of 2023.
16. C. John Carney. He scored 1,076 points from 1990 to 2000. Carney was selected to the Pro Bowl once with the Chargers, and again with the Giants in 2008. He also led the league in scoring during the 1994 season, when he was selected First-team All-Pro. He won a Super Bowl with the Saints during the 2009 season, just one year before he retired.
17. True. This includes the first Super Bowl.
18. True. They have 19 playoff berths, as of 2023.

Did You Know?

The Raiders and Broncos both have three Super Bowl victories, as of 2023.

CHAPTER 23:

NFC EAST

1. True or False: Troy Aikman has more passing yards than any other Cowboy, as of 2023.

2. True or False: Emmitt Smith is the only Cowboy with more than 10,000 rushing yards.

3. Which Cowboys receiver has caught more touchdown passes than any other Cowboy?

    A. Dez Bryant
    B. Jason Witten
    C. Bob Hayes
    D. Michael Irvin

4. Which Cowboys player has more points than any other Cowboy?

    A. Dan Bailey
    B. Rafael Septien
    C. Tony Dorsett
    D. Emmitt Smith

5. True or False: Eli Manning has 47,023 passing yards, the most in Giants history.

6. True or False: Tiki Barber is the only Giant to gather 10,000 rushing yards in team history.

7. Which Giants receiver leads the organization in yards and touchdown passes caught?

    A. Kyle Rote
    B. Joe Morrison
    C. Amani Toomer
    D. Odell Beckham Jr.

8. Which player leads the Giants in total interceptions?

    A. Jimmy Patton
    B. Spider Lockhart

C. Dick Lynch
D. Emlen Tunnell

9. True or False: Donovan McNabb leads the Eagles in all-time passing yards.

10. True or False: LeSean McCoy leads all Eagles rushers in yards and touchdowns.

11. Which Eagles receiver has the most receiving yards and touchdown passes caught?

    A. Harold Carmichael
    B. Pete Retzlaff
    C. DeSean Jackson
    D. Mike Quick

12. Which Eagles player has scored more points than any other player in team history?

    A. Bobby Walston
    B. David Akers
    C. Jake Elliott
    D. Sam Baker

13. True or False: Sonny Jurgensen leads all Washington Redskins (Commanders) in passing yards.

14. True or False: John Riggins has scored more rushing touchdowns than any other Redskins (Commanders) player in franchise history.

15. Which receiver has the most yards in Redskins (Commanders) history, but not touchdown receptions?

    A. Charley Taylor
    B. Santana Moss
    C. Gary Clark
    D. Art Monk

16. Which Redskins (Commanders) defender has more interceptions than any other player in team history?

    A. Brig Owens
    B. Sammy Baugh
    C. Darrell Green
    D. Mike Bass

17. True or False: The NFC East has 12 Super Bowl championships.
18. True or False: The Dallas Cowboys have 25 division titles, most among the NFC East.

CHAPTER 23 ANSWERS:

1. False. Tony Romo leads all Cowboys with 34,183 yards. Romo had to wait until 2006 to earn the full-time starting job, but he was selected to the Pro Bowl in his first full season as the starter. He would earn three more of those selections, and he would go on to lead the league in passer rating for the 2014 season.
2. False. Smith and Tony Dorsett both passed 10,000 yards.
3. A. Dez Bryant. He caught 73 touchdown passes from 2010 to 2017, earning three Pro Bowl selections. He led the league in touchdown catches in 2014.
4. D. Emmitt Smith. He is the rare non-kicker to lead his team in scoring.
5. False. Manning has 57,023 yards, the most in Giants history. Eli Manning played 16 seasons, all with the Giants. He is third on the list of quarterbacks for consecutive starts with 210. He helped the Giants win two Super Bowls, and he was named MVP on both of those occasions.
6. True. He got 10,449 yards from 1997 to 2006.
7. C. Amani Toomer. He had 54 touchdowns and 9,497 yards from 1996 to 2008.
8. D. Emlen Tunnell. He had 74 interceptions from 1948 to 1958.
9. True. McNabb had 32,873 yards from 1999 to 2009, which earned him six Pro Bowls and entry into the Philadelphia Eagles Hall of Fame.
10. False. McCoy has the most yards, but Steve Van Buren has the most touchdowns.
11. A. Harold Carmichael. He played from 1971 to 1983 with the Eagles. Carmichael was selected as the NFL Man of the Year in 1980, and he earned four Pro Bowl selections. In his 1973 season, he led the league in receiving yards and catches. He was inducted into the Philadelphia Eagles Hall of Fame.
12. B. David Akers. He scored 1,323 points from 1999 to 2010.
13. False. Joe Theismann is the franchise leader with 25,206 yards. Theismann and the Redskins (Commanders) won Super Bowl XVII, and he was named the NFL MVP for the 1983 season.
14. True. His 79 touchdowns are more than any Washington rusher.

15. D. Art Monk. He had 12,026 yards from 1980 to 1993. He earned three Pro Bowl selections to go with his three Super Bowl victories. He also led the NFL in catches during the 1984 season.
16. C. Darrell Green. He had 54 interceptions from 1983 to 2002.
17. False. As of 2023, the NFC East has 13 Super Bowl championships.
18. True. The Eagles are second with 12.

Did You Know?

As of 2023, no NFC East team has repeated as division champion since 2004.

CHAPTER 24:

NFC NORTH

1. True or False: Jay Cutler has the most passing yards of any Chicago Bears quarterback.

2. True or False: Walter Payton is the Bears' all-time leading rusher.

3. Which Bears player has more receiving yards than any other player in team history?

    A. Harlon Hill
    B. Alshon Jeffery
    C. Johnny Morris
    D. Walter Payton

4. Which Bears player has scored more points than any other Bear?

    A. Kevin Butler
    B. Robbie Gould
    C. Walter Payton
    D. Bob Thomas

5. True or False: No Detroit Lions quarterback has thrown for more yards, touchdowns, fumbles, and interceptions than Matthew Stafford.

6. True or False: Barry Sanders leads the Lions in all-time rushing yards.

7. Which Lions receiver leads the organization in receiving yards?

    A. Calvin Johnson
    B. Herman Moore
    C. Johnnie Morton
    D. Brett Perriman

8. Which Lions player is the all-time points leader for the team?

    A. Eddie Murray
    B. Barry Sanders
    C. Matt Prater
    D. Jason Hanson

9. True or False: Aaron Rodgers leads the Packers in all-time passing yards.

10. True or False: Ahman Green and Jim Taylor are the only Packers with more than 8,000 rushing yards.

11. Which Packers receiver is the only one to have more than 10,000 receiving yards?

    A. James Lofton
    B. Donald Driver
    C. Sterling Sharpe
    D. Davante Adams

12. Which Packers player has scored more points than any other Packer in team history?

    A. Ryan Longwell
    B. Don Hutson
    C. Mason Crosby
    D. Chris Jacke

13. True or False: Fran Tarkenton's 239 touchdown passes are the most of any Minnesota Viking.

14. True or False: Adrian Peterson had 9,747 yards for the Vikings, leading the organization.

15. Of all the talented receivers that have been with the Vikings, which player gathered the most yardage from catching passes?

    A. Cris Carter
    B. Randy Moss
    C. Anthony Carter
    D. Adam Thielen

16. Which player has scored more points for the Vikings than anyone else?

    A. Cris Carter
    B. Ryan Longwell
    C. Fred Cox
    D. Adrian Peterson

17. True or False: The Vikings have won the most NFC North titles as of 2023.

18. True or False: The Green Bay Packers are 4-1 in Super Bowl games.

CHAPTER 24 ANSWERS:

1. True. Cutler had 23,443 yards from 2009 to 2016.
2. True. Payton ran for 16,726 yards from 1975 to 1987. No other Bear has more than 10,000 yards. "Sweetness" won Super Bowl XX with the Bears, and he was named the league MVP in 1977. He also collected nine Pro Bowls and five First-team All-Pro selections. He's widely considered one of the best players of all time.
3. C. Johnny Morris. He had 5,059 yards from 1958 to 1967.
4. B. Robbie Gould. He scored 1,207 points from 2005 to 2015.
5. True. He leads the organization in each of those categories.
6. True. He has 10,000 more yards than the second-place Lions player, Billy Sims.
7. A. Calvin Johnson. He had 11,619 receiving yards from 2007 to 2015. "Megatron" only played seven seasons in the NFL before retiring, citing his physical health concerns. Despite his short career, he was inducted into the Hall of Fame in 2021.
8. D. Jason Hanson. He had 2,150 points from 1992 to 2012.
9. False. Brett Favre leads the organization in passing yards, with 61,655.
10. True. Green has 8,322 and Taylor has 8,207.
11. B. Donald Driver. His 10,137 yards were collected from 1999 to 2012. Those 14 seasons comprised the entirety of Driver's career, which included one Super Bowl championship and four Pro Bowl selections. He was also inducted into the Green Bay Packers Hall of Fame.
12. C. Mason Crosby. He scored 1,918 points from 2007 to 2022.
13. True. He also leads the organization in passing yards.
14. False. Peterson had 11,747 yards to lead the team all-time.
15. A. Cris Carter. He had 12,383 yards from 1990 to 2001. During his 12 seasons with the Vikings, he was selected to eight Pro Bowls. The Vikings have retired his number, 80, to honor Carter's contributions to the team during those years.
16. C. Fred Cox. He scored 1,365 points from 1963 to 1977.
17. True. They have 21 to Green Bay's 17.
18. True. They've only lost one Super Bowl they have reached.

Did You Know?

The Vikings have reached four Super Bowls as a member of the NFC Central/North, but they lost each time.

CHAPTER 25:

NFC SOUTH

1. True or False: Matt Ryan has more than double the passing yards of any other Falcons quarterback.

2. True or False: Gerald Riggs' 6,631 yards are good enough to top the list of Falcons running backs.

3. Which Falcons player leads the organization in career receiving touchdowns?

    A. Julio Jones
    B. Roddy White
    C. Terance Mathis
    D. Alfred Jenkins

4. Which Falcon has scored more points than any other Falcon in team history?

    A. Morten Andersen
    B. Younghoe Koo
    C. Mick Luckhurst
    D. Matt Bryant

5. True or False: Cam Newton has 15,000 more passing yards than Jake Delhomme as members of the Carolina Panthers.

6. True or False: The Panthers' all-time leading rushing yards leader is DeAngelo Williams.

7. Which Panther is the only one to gather more than 10,000 receiving yards?

    A. Muhsin Muhammad
    B. Greg Olsen
    C. D.J. Moore
    D. Steve Smith Sr.

8. Which Panther is the team's all-time leading scorer?

    A. John Kasay

B. Graham Gano
   C. Steve Smith Sr.
   D. Cam Newton

9. True or False: Archie Manning has the second-most yards for the Saints, behind Drew Brees.

10. True or False: Mark Ingram leads all Saints in rushing yards, with 6,500.

11. Which player has caught more touchdown passes than any other Saints player?
    A. Jimmy Graham
    B. Joe Horn
    C. Marques Colston
    D. Eric Martin

12. Which Saints have this kicker to thank for 1,318 points over 196 games?
    A. Wil Lutz
    B. Morten Andersen
    C. John Carney
    D. Doug Brien

13. True or False: Vinny Testaverde leads all Buccaneers quarterbacks in passing yards.

14. True or False: Warrick Dunn has the most rushing yards for the Buccaneers.

15. Only one Buccaneers receiver has more than 10,000 receiving yards. Who is it?
    A. Chris Godwin
    B. Mark Carrier
    C. Mike Evans
    D. Kevin House

16. Martin Gramatica leads all Buccaneers in scoring. Who is second?
    A. Mike Evans
    B. Michael Husted
    C. Connor Barth
    D. Mike Alstott

17. True or False: The 2021 Saints were the first team to ever sweep the NFC South during the regular season.

18. True or False: The NFC South is the only NFC division without a team from the 1960 merger.

CHAPTER 25 ANSWERS:

1. True. His 59,735 yards are more than double any other Falcons quarterback. "Matty Ice" played 14 seasons with the Falcons, earning four Pro Bowls and an NFL MVP award during his tenure. The team reached one Super Bowl but was unsuccessful.
2. True. Riggs gathered those yards from 1982 to 1988.
3. B. Roddy White. He caught 63 touchdown passes, three more than Jones.
4. D. Matt Bryant. He scored 1,163 points from 2009 to 2019.
5. False. Newton only passed for about 10,000 more yards than Delhomme. He also holds the NFL record for most rushing touchdowns by a quarterback, with 75. Newton was named the league MVP in 2015.
6. False. Jonathan Stewart leads all Panthers in rushing yards.
7. D. Steve Smith Sr. He had 12,197 yards from 2001 to 2013.
8. A. John Casay. He scored 1,482 points from 1995 to 2010.
9. True. Brees has 68,010 passing yards to Manning's 21,734. Drew Brees played 15 years in New Orleans, leading the team to a Super Bowl victory that also earned him a Super Bowl MVP. As a passer, he was prolific, leading the league in passing yards seven times, passing touchdowns four times, passer rating twice, and completion percentage six times.
10. True. He played 123 games for the team from 2011 to 2022.
11. C. Marques Colston. He had 72 touchdown catches from 2006 to 2015.
12. B. Morten Andersen. He played from 1982 to 1994.
13. False. Jameis Winston leads the organization with 19,737 yards in the air. Winston was selected to one Pro Bowl as a Buccaneer in 2015, and in his last season with the team, he led the league in passing yards.
14. False. James Wilder ran for 5,957 yards from 1981 to 1989, leading the organization.
15. C. Mike Evans. His 11,680 yards, as of 2023, are the most in team history.
16. A. Mike Evans. As of 2023, he is only 14 points from passing Gramatica.
17. True. They lost to the Buccaneers in the playoffs, though.

18. True. The Falcons are the oldest team in the group, and they joined the league in 1966.

Did You Know?

Each NFC South team has had at least four division titles since 2002, when the division was created.

CHAPTER 26:

NFC WEST

1. True or False: The Cardinals' all-time passing yards leader is Jake Plummer.

2. True or False: Ottis Anderson leads all Cardinals in rushing yards.

3. Only one Cardinals receiver has more than 9,000 receiving yards. Who?

    A. Roy Green
    B. Larry Fitzgerald
    C. Jackie Smith
    D. Anquan Boldin

4. Only one Cardinals player has scored more points than Larry Fitzgerald. Who?

    A. Jim Bakken
    B. Neil Rackers
    C. Greg Davis
    D. Neil O'Donoghue

5. True or False: Jim Everett has more passing yards than any other Rams player.

6. True or False: Steven Jackson is the only Rams player with more than 10,000 rushing yards.

7. Two Rams have had more than 10,000 receiving yards, as of 2023. Who has the most?

    A. Torry Holt
    B. Cooper Kupp
    C. Isaac Bruce
    D. Henry Ellard

8. Which Ram has the most points in team history?

    A. Greg Zuerlein
    B. Mike Lansford

C. Bob Waterfield
D. Jeff Wilkins

9. True or False: Joe Montana leads all 49ers quarterbacks in touchdown passes and passing yards.

10. True or False: Joe Perry is the only 49ers player to gather more than 10,000 rushing yards.

11. Which 49ers receiver has more than double the receiving yards, and double the touchdown passes, of the player in second place on the franchise list?

    A. Terrell Owens
    B. Jerry Rice
    C. Dwight Clark
    D. Gene Washington

12. Which 49ers player leads the organization in points scored?

    A. Jerry Rice
    B. Ray Wersching
    C. Tommy Davis
    D. Robbie Gould

13. True or False: Matt Hasselbeck leads all Seahawks quarterbacks in passing yards.

14. True or False: Shaun Alexander has more rushing yards than any other Seahawks player.

15. As of 2023, only one Seahawks player has more than 10,000 receiving yards. Who is it?

    A. Tyler Lockett
    B. Brian Blades
    C. Doug Baldwin
    D. Steve Largent

16. Which player has the most points while wearing a Seahawks uniform?

    A. Stephen Hauschka
    B. Shaun Alexander
    C. Norm Johnson
    D. Steve Largent

17. True or False: Before the AFL-NFL Merger in 1970, the NFC West was known as the NFL Coastal Division.

18. True or False: In 2010, the NFC West was the first division in league history to have a division champion with a losing record.

CHAPTER 26 ANSWERS:

1. False. The Cardinals' passing yards leader is Jim Hart. Hart played for the Cardinals from 1966 to 1983, throwing for 34,665 yards and 209 touchdowns. He had four Pro Bowl selections and was named to the Cardinals Ring of Honor.
2. True. He played from 1979 to 1986, gathering 7,999 yards.
3. B. Larry Fitzgerald. He had 17,492 yards from 2004 to 2020.
4. A. Jim Bakken. He scored 1,380 points from 1962 to 1978.
5. True. He had 23,758 yards from 1986 to 1993. Everett was only selected to one Pro Bowl, in 1990, but he led the league in passing touchdowns for the two seasons before his Pro Bowl selection.
6. True. He had 10,138 yards from 2004 to 2012.
7. C. Isaac Bruce. He had 14,109 yards from 1994 to 2007.
8. D. Jeff Wilkins. He had 1,223 points from 1997 to 2007.
9. True. He had 35,124 yards from 1979 to 1992. He also helped the 49ers win Super Bowls, three of which resulted in Super Bowl MVP selections. Montana was also selected to eight Pro Bowls in his career. To this day, he is tied for the most touchdowns in one playoff season, with 11.
10. False. Frank Gore is the only 49ers player to get 10,000 rushing yards. He had 11,073 yards.
11. B. Jerry Rice. He had 19,247 yards and 176 touchdowns while playing from 1985 to 2000.
12. A. Jerry Rice. He scored 1,130 points during his 238 games with the 49ers. That included three Super Bowl championships, one Super Bowl MVP, and 13 Pro Bowl selections. He led the entire league in scoring during the 1987 season. As of 2023, he holds 12 NFL records, including career receptions, receiving yards, and receiving touchdowns.
13. False. Russell Wilson leads the organization with 37,059 yards.
14. True. He had 9,429 yards from 2000 to 2007. His time with the Seahawks was productive enough to earn him a league MVP award in 2005. He also earned three Pro Bowl selections while playing with Seattle. During his MVP season, he led the league in scoring.
15. D. Steve Largent. He had 13,089 yards from 1976 to 1989.
16. C. Norm Johnson. He scored 810 points from 1982 to 1990.

17. True. The name changed in 1970, three years after its formation.
18. True. The Seahawks won the division with a 7-9 record.

DID YOU KNOW?

Since 1967, the 49ers have the most division championships, with the Rams in second place.

CHAPTER 27:

MVP SEASONS

1. True or False: Kurt Warner threw 38 touchdown passes in 1999 to earn the MVP.

2. True or False: In 1984, Dan Marino threw 48 touchdown passes and more than 5,000 passing yards to win the MVP.

3. Which quarterback won the MVP in 2007 with 50 touchdown passes, and over 300 passing yards per game?

   A. Drew Brees
   B. Peyton Manning
   C. Eli Manning
   D. Tom Brady

4. Which quarterback set a new passer rating record of 112.4 in 1989, winning the MVP?

   A. Jack Trudeau
   B. Joe Montana
   C. Troy Aikman
   D. Jim McMahon

5. True or False: Troy Aikman broke Joe Montana's passer rating record in 1994 to win the MVP.

6. True or False: As of 2023, Aaron Rodgers' MVP season in 2011 set the current passer rating record.

7. Which quarterback won the MVP in 2013, throwing 55 touchdown passes?

   A. Aaron Rodgers
   B. Philip Rivers
   C. Drew Brees
   D. Peyton Manning

8. In 2006, which running back posted 31 total touchdowns and 2,323 yards to win the MVP?

A. Adrian Peterson
   B. LaDainian Tomlinson
   C. Brian Westbrook
   D. Willie Parker

9. True or False: In 1998, Terrell Davis averaged more than five yards per carry and scored 21 rushing touchdowns to win the MVP.

10. True or False: Lawrence Taylor was the first defensive player to win the MVP award, which he earned in 1986.

11. Which player missed the first two games of the 1993 season but still led the league in rushing yards, winning the MVP?

    A. Emmitt Smith
    B. Jerome Bettis
    C. Thurman Thomas
    D. Barry Sanders

12. Cam Newton won the MVP in 2015 by figuring in how many of his team's 54 offensive touchdowns?

    A. 42
    B. 45
    C. 47
    D. 49

13. True or False: O.J. Simpson was the first player in history to rush for more than 2,000 yards in a season, winning the 1973 season MVP.

14. True or False: Walter Payton broke O.J. Simpson's record for total scrimmage yards in 1977, winning the MVP in the process.

15. Which running back won the MVP in 2012 with 2,097 rushing yards?

    A. Arian Foster
    B. Doug Martin
    C. Adrian Peterson
    D. Marshawn Lynch

16. Peyton Manning won the MVP in 2004 but didn't lead the league in which category?

    A. Passing yards
    B. Touchdown passes
    C. Passer rating

D. First down passes
17. True or False: Two players shared the NFL MVP in 1997, and they played two different positions.
18. True or False: In 2010, Tom Brady threw 36 touchdowns and only five interceptions to win MVP.

CHAPTER 27 ANSWERS:

1. False. He threw 41 touchdown passes, won the MVP, and won the Super Bowl.
2. True. His numbers set a ton of records until the game adapted to more throwing.
3. D. Tom Brady. It was a perfect regular season, but they lost in the Super Bowl.
4. B. Joe Montana. He didn't win MVP at the Super Bowl, though.
5. False. Steve Young broke Montana's record on his way to an MVP award.
6. True. The current record is 122.5.
7. True. Manning's Broncos were blown out in the Super Bowl, though.
8. B. LaDainian Tomlinson. As of 2023, it is still the record for most total touchdowns in a season.
9. True. He had 2,008 yards on the ground and helped Denver win the Super Bowl.
10. False. He was the second defensive player to earn it. Alan Page won it in 1971.
11. A. Emmitt Smith. He had 1,486 yards and helped Dallas win the Super Bowl.
12. B. 45. He had 35 in the air and ten on the ground.
13. True. Simpson averaged 143.1 yards per game.
14. True. Payton had 2,121 scrimmage yards that season.
15. C. Adrian Peterson. He only had 13 total touchdowns that year, though.
16. A. Passing yards. Daunte Culpepper led the league in that category.
17. True. Brett Favre and Barry Sanders tied for the most votes and split the award.
18. False. He only threw four.

Did You Know?

Peyton Manning has five AP NFL MVP awards, more than any other player.

CHAPTER 28:
NFL CHAMPIONSHIPS

1. True or False: The Cowboys beat the Steelers in Super Bowl XIII, as Roger Staubach outdueled Terry Bradshaw.

2. True or False: The Helmet Catch helped the Giants defeat the Patriots in Super Bowl XLII.

3. Malcolm Butler intercepted which quarterback's pass to help the Patriots win Super Bowl XLIX?
   A. Matt Ryan
   B. Russell Wilson
   C. Eli Manning
   D. Cam Newton

4. The Patriots overcame which of these deficits to win Super Bowl LI?
   A. 24-3
   B. 21-0
   C. 28-3
   D. 27-7

5. True or False: In Super Bowl XXV, the Giants won thanks to the infamous "Wide Left" field goal.

6. True or False: Nick Foles led the Eagles over the Patriots in a shootout to win Super Bowl LII.

7. Which team came up one yard short of an epic comeback against the St. Louis Rams in Super Bowl XXXIV?
   A. Tennessee Titans
   B. New England Patriots
   C. Buffalo Bills
   D. Baltimore Ravens

8. Which Steelers receiver made an incredible catch in the corner of the end zone, helping them win Super Bowl XLIII?
   A. Hines Ward

B. Heath Miller
   C. Nate Washington
   D. Santonio Holmes

9. True or False: Tom Brady helped New England defeat the Rams in Super Bowl XXXVI in his first full season as a starter.

10. True or False: John Elway won his first Super Bowl by defeating the Chicago Bears in Super Bowl XXXII.

11. A 34-minute power outage almost helped which team come back against the Ravens in Super Bowl XLVII?

    A. San Francisco 49ers
    B. Los Angeles Rams
    C. Green Bay Packers
    D. New York Giants

12. Which team used an onside kick to start the second half of Super Bowl XLIV, helping them to a victory over the Colts?

    A. Dallas Cowboys
    B. New Orleans Saints
    C. Tampa Bay Buccaneers
    D. Seattle Seahawks

13. True or False: Clay Matthews hit Hines Ward, causing a turnover and helping the Packers beat the Steelers in Super Bowl XLV.

14. True or False: Terrell Owens and Donovan McNabb couldn't help the Eagles overcome the Colts to win Super Bowl XXXIX.

15. Desmond Howard returned a kick during Super Bowl XXXI, helping the Packers beat which team?

    A. New England Patriots
    B. Denver Broncos
    C. Indianapolis Colts
    D. Miami Dolphins

16. The Dolphins completed their perfect season by defeating which team in Super Bowl VII?

    A. San Francisco 49ers
    B. Washington Redskins (Commanders)
    C. Green Bay Packers

D. Dallas Cowboys
17. True or False: Super Bowl 50 did not use Roman numerals, as it would have only been the letter L.
18. True or False: The Redskins (Commanders) set a Super Bowl record with 35 points in the second quarter of Super Bowl XXII.

CHAPTER 28 ANSWERS:

1. False. Bradshaw and the Steelers defeated the Cowboys 35-31.
2. True. David Tyree's career is defined by that catch, which spoiled the perfect season for the New England Patriots.
3. B. Russell Wilson. The goal line stand was the defining moment of that contest. The play call was considered controversial, as the Seahawks did not utilize their power running back, Marshawn Lynch, in a goal line situation.
4. C. 28-3. It was also the first Super Bowl to require overtime.
5. False. It was the "Wide Right" field goal attempt that gave the Giants the win.
6. True. The final score was 41-33.
7. A. Tennessee Titans. The final score was 23-16. On the final play of the game, Steve McNair completed a pass to Kevin Dyson, who needed to reach the end zone to possibly tie the game. He was tackled as he reached out for the goal line, but he came up a yard short. It was one of the most dramatic finishes in NFL history.
8. D. Santonio Holmes. The Steelers won 27-23.
9. True. The Patriots won 20-17.
10. False. Elway and the Broncos defeated the Packers.
11. A. San Francisco 49ers. The 49ers were down by 22, and only lost by three.
12. B. New Orleans Saints. The Saints won 31-17.
13. False. Matthews hit Rashard Mendenhall to cause the turnover.
14. False. The Eagles lost to the Patriots in that Super Bowl.
15. A. New England Patriots. The Packers won 35-21.
16. B. Washington Redskins (Commanders). The final score was 14-7.
17. True. The league also wanted to emphasize the 50th anniversary.
18. True. They beat the Broncos 42-10.

DID YOU KNOW?

The Steelers and Patriots both have six Super Bowl wins, as of 2023.

CHAPTER 29:

FOOTBALL HALL OF FAME

1. True or False: The Chicago Bears have 32 players in the Hall of Fame, the most of any NFL team.

2. True or False: The Jacksonville Jaguars were the last team to get one of their players into the Hall of Fame.

3. The first full-time punter was inducted as part of which class year?

   A. 1994
   B. 2004
   C. 2014
   D. 2024

4. Devin Hester was the first primary return specialist to be inducted, which happened during which class year?

   A. 1994
   B. 2004
   C. 2014
   D. 2024

5. True or False: As part of the charter class in 1963, 20 inductees were selected.

6. True or False: Dwight Freeney, inducted in 2024, played for six different teams during his career.

7. Which player, along with Chuck Bednarik, was the first to be inducted in his first year of eligibility, back in 1967?

   A. Ken Strong
   B. Art Donovan
   C. Bobby Layne
   D. Hugh McElhenney

8. Four people were elected to the Hall in 1972. Which one was a quarterback?

   A. Lamar Hunt

B. Ace Parker
   C. Gino Marchetti
   D. Ollie Matson

9. True or False: Johnny Unitas was elected to the Hall of Fame in 1979, his second year of eligibility.

10. True or False: Joe Namath was elected to the Hall in his first year of eligibility, 1985.

11. Which of these players, all elected to the Hall in 1988, was in their first year of eligibility?

    A. Fred Biletnikoff
    B. Mike Ditka
    C. Jack Ham
    D. Alan Page

12. Of the four individuals selected in 1992, only one was not a player. Who?

    A. Al Davis
    B. John Mackey
    C. John Riggins
    D. Lem Barney

13. True or False: Jimmy Johnson was inducted into the Hall of Fame for playing safety with the 49ers.

14. True or False: Legendary coach Don Shula was inducted into the Hall of Fame in 1997 for his time with the Dolphins and Colts.

15. Which quarterback entered the Hall of Fame in 2000?

    A. Dan Fouts
    B. Joe Montana
    C. Jim Kelly
    D. John Elway

16. Which of these players was inducted into the Hall of Fame first?

    A. Dan Marino
    B. Steve Young
    C. Barry Sanders
    D. Warren Moon

17. True or False: Deion Sanders finished his Hall of Fame career with the Washington Redskins (Commanders).

18. True or False: Randy Moss and Terrell Owens were both voted into the Hall of Fame in 2018.

CHAPTER 29 ANSWERS:

1. True. The first Chicago Bears player inducted was George Halas, the founder of the team.
2. True. Tony Boselli was inducted in 2022.
3. C. 2014. Ray Guy of the Raiders was that punter.
4. D. 2024. No other player has yet to earn Hall of Fame honors playing that position as their primary position.
5. False. The charter class was 17 members, selected in 1963, the first year in which inductees were selected.
6. True. He is one of the rare modern inductees to have played for so many teams.
7. C. Bobby Layne. He played for four teams, spending most of his time with the Lions.
8. B. Ace Parker. He played for the Brooklyn Dodgers from 1937 to 1941.
9. False. He was elected to the Hall in his first year of eligibility.
10. False. He was elected in 1985, but it was not his first year of eligibility.
11. C. Jack Ham. He played with the Steelers as a linebacker from 1971 to 1982.
12. A. Al Davis. He was a coach, GM, and owner of the Raiders.
13. False. He played cornerback, not safety.
14. True. He coached from 1963 to 1995.
15. B. Joe Montana. He played for the 49ers and Chiefs.
16. C. Barry Sanders. He was in 2004, one year before Young and Marino, and two years before Moon.
17. False. He played for the Ravens from 2004 to 2005.
18. True. Both players played for five teams during their time in the league.

Did You Know?

As of 2024, the number of players inducted into the Hall of Fame during their first year of eligibility is 76.

CHAPTER 30:

UNBEATABLE RECORDS

1. True or False: Derrick Thomas recorded seven sacks in a November 1990 game against the Seahawks.

2. True or False: Michael Thomas caught 151 passes in 2019, a record.

3. Since 1970, which team holds the record for most consecutive losses?

   A. Detroit Lions
   B. Cleveland Browns
   C. Tampa Bay Buccaneers
   D. Houston Texans

4. Who is the only player to play 26 seasons in the league?

   A. George Blanda
   B. Morten Andersen
   C. Adam Vinatieri
   D. Tom Brady

5. True or False: The San Francisco 49ers won 21 straight road games from 1988 to 1990.

6. True or False: Brett Favre holds the NFL record with 297 straight games started.

7. Only one quarterback has thrown eight interceptions in one game. Who was it?

   A. Ty Detmer
   B. Ken Stabler
   C. Ryan Fitzpatrick
   D. Jim Hardy

8. Paul Krause holds the NFL record with how many career interceptions?

   A. 76
   B. 79
   C. 81

D. 84

9. True or False: In 1945, Packers wide receiver Don Hutson scored 29 points in one quarter.

10. True or False: Willie Anderson had 336 receiving yards in a game against the Saints in 1989.

11. Which player holds the record for most passing yards in a game?

   A. Y.A. Tittle
   B. Norm Van Brocklin
   C. Vince Ferragamo
   D. Phil Simms

12. Which running back has the most rushing yards in a single game?

   A. Adrian Peterson
   B. O.J. Simpson
   C. Walter Payton
   D. LaDainian Tomlinson

13. True or False: Drew Brees has 16 400-yard passing games, more than any other quarterback.

14. True or False: Jerry Rice holds the record for most career receptions.

15. Jerry Rice also leads in receiving yards. How many more does he have than Larry Fitzgerald?

   A. 3,100
   B. 3,845
   C. 5,403
   D. 6,115

16. Jerry Rice also leads in receiving touchdowns. Who is second on that list?

   A. Terrell Owens
   B. Randy Moss
   C. Cris Carter
   D. Marvin Harrison

17. True or False: Adrian Peterson holds the single season rushing record with 2,097 yards.

18. True or False: With 18,355 yards, Emmitt Smith holds the career rushing yards record.

CHAPTER 30 ANSWERS:

1. True. Other players have only reached 5.5 sacks three times since then.
2. False. He only caught 149, but it's still the record.
3. C. Tampa Bay Buccaneers. They lost 26 straight games in 1976 and 1977.
4. A. George Blanda. He played both quarterback and kicker.
5. False. They only won 18 road games in a row, but it's still the record.
6. True. Philip Rivers is the next closest quarterback, but his streak ended at 240.
7. D. Jim Hardy. He threw eight back in 1950. Detmer and Stabler threw seven, and Fitzpatrick threw six.
8. C. 81. He played for Washington and Minnesota from 1964 to 1979.
9. True. He scored four touchdowns and kicked five PATs.
10. True. His team won in overtime.
11. B. Norm Van Brocklin. He had 554 passing yards in a 1951 game against the New York Yanks.
12. A. Adrian Peterson. He had 296 yards against the Chargers in 2007.
13. True. Tom Brady and Peyton Manning both have 14 games each.
14. True. He had 1,549 catches, over 100 more than the second-place Larry Fitzgerald.
15. C. 5,403. His 22,895 yards are significantly more than Fitzgerald's 17,492.
16. B. Randy Moss. He had 156 touchdowns to Rice's 197.
17. False. Peterson had that many yards in 2007, but Eric Dickerson had 2,105 yards in 1984.
18. True. Walter Payton is in second place with 16,726 yards.

Did You Know?

Don Shula has more coaching victories than anyone else, with 347.

CHAPTER 31:

THE BIGGEST MOMENTS

1. True or False: "The Immaculate Reception" helped the Steelers defeat the Raiders during the 1972 playoffs.

2. True or False: John Madden was the coach of the Raiders, who lost due to "The Immaculate Reception" play.

3. "The Catch," a legendary play from 1982, was caught by which receiver?

    A. Tony Dorsett
    B. Earl Cooper
    C. Dwight Clark
    D. Freddie Solomon

4. "The Catch" took place during which phase of the 1981 playoffs?

    A. NFC Wild Card
    B. NFC Divisional
    C. NFC Championship
    D. Super Bowl

5. True or False: "The Music City Miracle" featured only one lateral pass.

6. True or False: "The Music City Miracle" helped the Titans win the AFC Divisional over the Bills.

7. "The Helmet Catch" was caught by which receiver?

    A. Plaxico Burress
    B. David Tyree
    C. Amani Toomer
    D. Steve Smith

8. The play before "The Helmet Catch," which Patriots cornerback dropped a game-winning interception?

    A. Ellis Hobbs
    B. Randall Gay

C. James Sanders
   D. Asante Samuel

9. True or False: "The Miracle in Miami" was the first multiple lateral-pass touchdown to win a game in NFL history.

10. True or False: Rob Gronkowski was playing defense when "The Miracle in Miami" took place.

11. Which Steeler took an interception 100 yards in Super Bowl XLIII?

    A. James Harrison
    B. James Farrior
    C. LaMarr Woodley
    D. Troy Polamalu

12. "The Miracle at the Meadowlands" took place between the Giants and which team?

    A. Broncos
    B. Browns
    C. Eagles
    D. Bears

13. True or False: "The Miracle at the Meadowlands" winning touchdown was scored by Herman Edwards.

14. True or False: "The Drive" took place during the 1987 AFC Championship Game between the Broncos and Browns.

15. One year after "The Drive," the Cleveland Browns made which iconic play in the 1987 AFC Championship Game?

    A. "The Hail Mary"
    B. "The Fumble"
    C. "The Sack"
    D. "The Interception"

16. "Wide Right" was a field goal missed by which kicker in 1991?

    A. John Kasay
    B. Scott Norwood
    C. Pete Stoyanovich
    D. Pat Leahy

17. True or False: The 1972 Dolphins finished their perfect season by beating the Redskins (Commanders) in the Super Bowl.

18. True or False: "Garo's Gaffe" cost the Dolphins Super Bowl VIII.

CHAPTER 31 ANSWERS:

1. True. Franco Harris caught the pass and scored the winning touchdown.
2. True. Many thought the catch was illegal at the time, but it still stood.
3. C. Dwight Clark. He could not have jumped any higher to make the play.
4. C. NFC Championship. The 49ers defeated the Cowboys 28-27.
5. True. There was one handoff and one lateral pass during the crazy end to the game.
6. False. The Titans won the AFC Wild Card game against the Bills.
7. B. David Tyree. His catch helped defeat the undefeated Patriots.
8. D. Asante Samuel. NFL history was nearly rewritten in that moment.
9. True. It only took two laterals, but the Dolphins used them well.
10. True. The Patriots had anticipated a Hail Mary, and it cost them.
11. A. James Harrison. The touchdown helped the Steelers defeat the Cardinals.
12. C. Eagles. The Eagles won thanks to the unforced error from the Giants.
13. True. He picked up the botched handoff and ran it back for the touchdown.
14. True. The Broncos drove the ball 98 yards in five minutes to tie the game.
15. B. "The Fumble." They lost to the Broncos again.
16. B. Scott Norwood. His kick cost the Bills the Super Bowl.
17. True. They won the game 14-7.
18. False. "Garo's Gaffe" nearly cost the Dolphins Super Bowl VII, their perfect season.

Did You Know?

"The Ice Bowl," in 1967, was won by the Packers, defeating the Cowboys, and giving Green Bay their third straight championship.

CHAPTER 32:

SUPER BOWL MVPS

1. True or False: Tom Brady threw for 366 yards to help the Patriots defeat the Falcons in Super Bowl LI.

2. True or False: Steve Young won the Super Bowl MVP one year after the 49ers let Joe Montana go.

3. How many catches did Jerry Rice need to gather 215 receiving yards and the Super Bowl MVP in 1988?
   A. 11
   B. 12
   C. 13
   D. 14

4. Which quarterback led the "Greatest Show on Turf" to win the Super Bowl XXXIV MVP?
   A. Peyton Manning
   B. Brett Favre
   C. Drew Bledsoe
   D. Kurt Warner

5. True or False: The first Black quarterback to win the Super Bowl was Doug Washington, and he also won the Super Bowl MVP with the championship.

6. True or False: Terrell Davis was a sixth-round pick who went on to win Super Bowl XXXII MVP.

7. Which quarterback threw for 331 yards and three touchdowns in Super Bowl XIX to claim the MVP?
   A. Jim McMahon
   B. Dan Marino
   C. Troy Aikman
   D. Joe Montana

8. Which player was the Super Bowl MVP when the Giants spoiled the Patriots' bid for a perfect season?

    A. David Tyree
    B. Eli Manning
    C. Tom Brady
    D. Plaxico Burress

9. True or False: Joe Montana won the Super Bowl XXIV MVP with 297 yards and four touchdowns.

10. True or False: The Jets' only Super Bowl victory came thanks to MVP Joe Namath.

11. How many carries did Marcus Allen need to score two touchdowns and gain 191 yards in Super Bowl XVIII?

    A. 16
    B. 20
    C. 22
    D. 25

12. How many touchdown passes did Tom Brady throw against Seattle's "Legion of Boom" to win the MVP during Super Bowl XLIX?

    A. 2
    B. 3
    C. 4
    D. 5

13. True or False: Lynn Swann was the first wide receiver to win the Super Bowl MVP during Super Bowl X.

14. True or False: Nick Foles threw for three touchdowns and caught a touchdown pass in Super Bowl LII.

15. Terry Bradshaw threw how many touchdowns during his Super Bowl XIII MVP performance?

    A. Two
    B. Three
    C. Four
    D. Five

16. Which quarterback was named MVP in Super Bowl I?

A. Bart Starr
B. Johnny Unitas
C. Len Dawson
D. Sonny Jurgensen

17. True or False: Phil Simms threw three touchdowns to help the Giants beat the Broncos in Super Bowl XXI.

18. True or False: Troy Aikman had three touchdowns and 273 yards to win Super Bowl XXVII.

CHAPTER 32 ANSWERS:

1. False. He threw for 466 yards and earned the Super Bowl MVP.
2. True. He helped the 49ers beat the Chargers in Super Bowl XXIX.
3. A. 11. The 49ers beat the Bengals to win Super Bowl XXIII.
4. D. Kurt Warner. He had 414 yards and two touchdowns against the Titans.
5. True. He had 340 yards and four touchdowns.
6. True. He had 157 yards on the ground and three touchdowns.
7. D. Joe Montana. His 49ers beat the Dolphins to win the Super Bowl.
8. B. Eli Manning. He had 255 yards in the air to win the game 17-14.
9. False. He had five touchdowns.
10. True. He threw for 206 yards in the contest.
11. B. 20. He helped the Raiders to a 38-9 victory.
12. C. Four. He also had two interceptions, but winning the Super Bowl helped him earn the MVP.
13. True. He had four catches for 161 yards, including a 64-yard touchdown.
14. True. The "Philly Special" helped his team defeat the Patriots.
15. C. Four. His Steelers defeated the Cowboys 35-31.
16. A. Bart Starr. He had two touchdown passes and 250 yards against the Chiefs.
17. True. Simms' Giants scored 17 points in the third quarter alone.
18. False. Aikman had four touchdowns to help the Cowboys destroy the Bills, 52-17.

DID YOU KNOW?

Tom Brady is the only player with five Super Bowl MVPs. No one has four. Joe Montana and Patrick Mahomes each have three.

CHAPTER 33:

SCANDALS AND MODERN HEADLINES

1. True or False: The 1925 Chicago Cardinals won the NFL Championship after the Pottsville Maroons were suspended at the end of the season.

2. True or False: Alex Karras and Paul Hornung were both suspended for sports betting in 1963, and neither made it to the Hall of Fame.

3. Which Steelers coach was sued by a Raiders player, then again by one of his own players, after he insinuated that they were both part of a "criminal element" in the NFL?

   A. Chuck Noll
   B. Buddy Parker
   C. Bill Cowher
   D. Mike Tomlin

4. Which team infamously escaped their old city in the middle of the night?

   A. Rams
   B. Raiders
   C. Chargers
   D. Colts

5. True or False: The Patriots had to forfeit two first-round picks for taping opponents' practices in 2007.

6. True or False: The 2014 Patriots had to give up two picks, and Tom Brady was suspended four games, for deflating footballs to their advantage.

7. Which player served 21 months in federal prison for operating a dogfighting ring?

   A. Brett Favre
   B. Tony Romo

C. Michael Vick
   D. Donovan McNabb

8. Which team was punished for offering financial rewards for injuring opponents during playoff games in 2009?

   A. New England Patriots
   B. New Orleans Saints
   C. New York Giants
   D. New York Jets

9. True or False: Ray Rice was suspended indefinitely for a domestic violence scandal in 2014.

10. True or False: Colin Kaepernick sparked controversy by kneeling to protest police violence against Black people.

11. Peyton Manning suffered a neck injury in 2011, leading to the Colts cutting him in 2012. Who signed him?

    A. Denver Broncos
    B. San Diego Chargers
    C. Oakland Raiders
    D. Chicago Bears

12. What constitutes a catch in the NFL was mired in controversy when which wide receiver was denied a game-winning touchdown in 2010?

    A. Dez Bryant
    B. Chad Johnson
    C. Terrell Owens
    D. Calvin Johnson

13. True or False: "The Fail Mary" was a controversial play that led to replacement referees being brought into the league.

14. True or False: Andrew Luck retired from the NFL after several injuries, ending his career in 2019.

15. Which team became the first to leave its original market twice when they moved away in 2020?

    A. Chargers
    B. Rams
    C. Raiders
    D. Cardinals

16. Which star running back did not play in 2018 because of a contract dispute?
    A. Todd Gurley
    B. Le'Veon Bell
    C. Alvin Kamara
    D. Kareem Hunt

17. True or False: Aaron Rodgers injured his Achilles only a few minutes into the season with his new team, the New York Jets.

18. True or False: Damar Hamlin returned to football after suffering a cardiac arrest during a game against the Bengals.

CHAPTER 33 ANSWERS:

1. True. The Cardinals quickly scheduled two more games against weak opponents to get more wins and pass Pottsville in the standings.
2. False. Both were reinstated and eventually made it to the Hall of Fame.
3. A. Chuck Noll. Noll won the first lawsuit, and his own player dropped the second one.
4. D. Colts. The city of Baltimore even tried to claim eminent domain over the team.
5. False. They only had to give up one first-round pick.
6. True. "Deflategate" was a scandal, but many wonder if it had that much of an effect against the Colts, whom the Patriots blew out in the AFC Championship Game, 45-7.
7. C. Michael Vick. He returned to the league after his sentence and even made a Pro Bowl.
8. B. New Orleans Saints. Coach Sean Payton was suspended but later reinstated.
9. True. His initial suspension was two games, but then a video of the incident was released, and his suspension was updated.
10. True. He eventually left the league when no team would sign him due the controversy around the protest.
11. A. Denver Broncos. Manning and the Broncos would win the Super Bowl just three years later.
12. D. Calvin Johnson. The ball came out of his hand as he went to ground against the Bears.
13. False. The replacement referees botched the call while the usual referees were in a lockout.
14. True. His retirement was a shock to the NFL, as he was one of the top players in the league when healthy.
15. C. Raiders. They moved to Las Vegas in 2020.
16. B. Le'Veon Bell. He got a four-year deal worth $52.5 million when he returned in 2019.
17. True. He did not play for the rest of the 2023 season.
18. True. He had a condition called commotio cordis, but he recovered and returned to the field.

DID YOU KNOW?

Tom Brady and J.J. Watt both retired in 2023.

CHAPTER 34:
FOOTBALL STATISTICS AND ACRONYMS

1. YDS. It's an indicator of success, but not necessarily winning.
2. 4QC. They're thrilling for the winning team when it happens.
3. GWD. The most exciting part of the game, sometimes.
4. Y/C. Short ones aren't as valuable to the team as long ones.
5. 2PM. It's not the time, but it might mean it's time for a comeback.
6. FF. It's a good thing for defenders.
7. INT. It doesn't mean integers, but it could be good or bad, depending on which side of the play you're on.
8. R/G. You can gather a lot of these, and the only things it means are that you run good routes and have good hands.
9. Sk%. If this number is high, the quarterback is likely injured often.
10. TD%. Not all of them have to be scores, but it would be great if they were.
11. XPM. This number should always be high for kickers.
12. SoS. If a team has a difficult one, they might need to make an SOS call for help.
13. Tkl. Only one of these can be made per play.
14. Pnt. The offense doesn't want to do this because their drive ends.
15. A/G. It basically represents how often a player participates in a play.
16. D/ST. You'll see this acronym in many fantasy football leagues.
17. -20. It's a great thing for the special teams.
18. SOLO. The best defenders don't need help.

CHAPTER 34 ANSWERS:

1. Yards. If you're gaining yards, you're doing well.
2. Fourth quarter comeback. Quarterbacks with lots of these are fun to watch.
3. Game-winning drives. Clutch quarterbacks can take over a game with very little time left.
4. Yards gained per pass completion. However, shorter passes are more reliable.
5. Two-point conversions made. You know when you need a tiny bit more to close the gap.
6. Forced fumbles. It is one of the most valuable plays a defender can make.
7. Interceptions. Quarterbacks don't want to commit these, and defenders love to get these.
8. Receptions per game. You have to get open and make the catch.
9. Sack percentage. Big numbers could also mean a problem with the offensive line.
10. Touchdown percentage. Some quarterbacks like to go big on every play.
11. Extra points made. It has become more difficult in recent years but still expected.
12. Strength of schedule. A difficult schedule can make for a long season.
13. Tackles. This stat was made official in 1994.
14. Punts. Punters can play a vital role in the game, though.
15. Attempts per game. It can be used to track runs and throws.
16. Defense/special teams. It represents the non-offensive players on a team.
17. Punts inside the 20-yard line. It helps the defense get a leg up on the opponent.
18. Solo tackles. Most tackles are made as a group, so it's special when a player does it on their own.

DID YOU KNOW?

The sack was not an official statistic in football until 1982.

CONCLUSION

Time has expired on this exciting contest! Did you kneel down to a comfortable victory? Perhaps you needed a last-second field goal to seal the deal or an exciting game-winning drive. Either way, the hope is that you enjoyed the trivia questions in this book.

If you struggled with some chapters, don't worry! This book covers a lot of ground in terms of football teams and decades of football events. You may need to revisit some of these chapters again to see if you can get the answers right next time. You can also look deeper into some of the names and events you learned about from these questions.

We talked about some of the best players from each of the NFL's 32 teams, including their top quarterbacks and running backs. Some teams have not had the luxury of a franchise player with impressive numbers on the stat sheet, but it doesn't take away from their importance to that organization and their fans.

Football is a great sport, and many excellent players have given their all on the field. You may not have had the opportunity to explore every team in depth, but hopefully these questions have piqued your interest in players and teams you haven't explored before.

You may not have been a fan of Tom Brady or Emmitt Smith before playing through this trivia book, for example. There is no denying, though, the impact that these kinds of players have had on the sport. Even the founders of the game have their place in this book, as the sport would not exist without their efforts.

If you enjoyed this book, share it with friends and family. Quiz your friends to prove you're the ultimate football master. Ask your family members if they know who has the most rushing yards in a season, or who has played the most games in a row.

It's a great way to share your favorite sport with the people you care about most.

Thank you for reading and be sure to keep both hands on the book until you complete the catch!

www.ingramcontent.com/pod-product-compliance
Lightning Source LLC
Chambersburg PA
CBHW060501030426
42337CB00015B/1686